Compilation of Key Documents
of the Antarctic Treaty System

Fifth edition

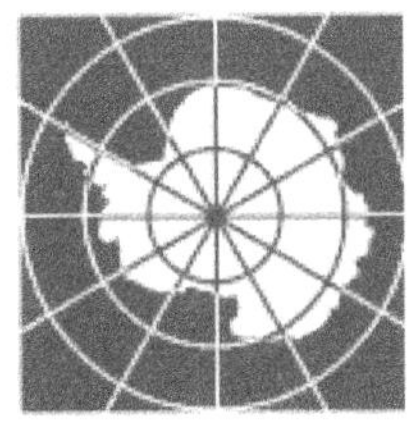

Secretariat of the Antarctic Treaty
Secrétariat du Traité sur l'Antarctique
Секретариат Договора об Антарктике
Secretaría del Tratado Antártico

Compilation of Key Documents
of the Antarctic Treaty System

Fifth edition

Secretariat of the Antarctic Treaty
Buenos Aires
2021

COMPILATION of key documents of the Antarctic Treaty system.
Fifth edition

Buenos Aires : Secretariat of the Antarctic Treaty, 2021.
196 p.
ISBN 978-987-8929-09-5
1. International law. 2. Antarctic Treaty System. 3. International
agreements.
DDC 341.2/9

CONTENTS

ANTARCTIC TREATY

WASHINGTON, D.C. - OCTOBER 15, 1959

December 1, 1959

FINAL ACT

ACTE FINAL

ЗАКЛЮЧИТЕЛЬНЫЙ АКТ

ACTA FINAL

FINAL ACT

The Governments of Argentina, Australia, Belgium, Chile, the French Republic, Japan, New Zealand, Norway, the Union of South Africa, the Union of Soviet Socialist Republics, the United Kingdom of Great Britain and Northern Ireland, and the United States of America,

Having accepted the invitation extended to them on May 2, 1958, by the Government of the United States of America to participate in a Conference on Antarctica to be attended by representatives of the twelve nations which cooperated in the Antarctic Program of the International Geophysical Year;

Appointed their respective Representatives, who are listed below by countries:

<u>Argentina</u>

<u>Representative</u>

His Excellency
Adolfo Scilingo
(Head of Delegation)

<u>Alternate Representative</u>

Dr. Francisco R. Bello

Australia

Representatives

    The Right Honorable
Richard Gardiner Casey, C.H., D.S.O., M.C., M.P.
(Head of Delegation)

    His Excellency the Honorable
Howard Beale, Q.C.
(Deputy Head of Delegation)

Alternate Representatives

    J. C. G. Kevin

    M. R. Booker

Belgium

Representative

    His Excellency
Viscount Obert de Thieusies
(Head of Delegation)

Alternate Representatives

    Jean de Bassompierre

    Alfred van der Essen

Chile

Representatives

    His Excellency
Marcial Mora
(Head of Delegation)

    His Excellency
Enrique Gajardo

    His Excellency
Julio Escudero

Alternate Representative

    Horacio Suarez

<u>The French Republic</u>

<u>Representative</u>

> His Excellency
> Pierre Charpentier
> (Head of Delegation)

<u>Alternate Representative</u>

> Guy Scalabre

<u>Japan</u>

<u>Representatives</u>

> His Excellency
> Koichiro Asakai
> (Head of Delegation)
>
> Takeso Shimoda

<u>New Zealand</u>

<u>Representatives</u>

> The Right Honorable
> Walter Nash, C.H.
> (Head of Delegation)
>
> A. D. McIntosh, C.M.G.
> (Deputy Head of Delegation)

<u>Alternate Representative</u>

> G. D. L. White, M.V.O.

<u>Norway</u>

<u>Representatives</u>

> His Excellency
> Paul Koht
> (Head of Delegation)
>
> Torfinn Oftedal
> (Deputy Head of Delegation)

<u>Alternate Representatives</u>

> Dr. Anders K. Orvin
>
> Gunnar Haerum

Union of South Africa

Representatives

The Honorable
Eric H. Louw
(Head of Delegation)

His Excellency
W. C. du Plessis
(Deputy Head of Delegation)

Alternate Representatives

J. G. Stewart

A. G. Dunn

D. Stuart Franklin

Union of Soviet Socialist Republics

Representatives

His Excellency
Vasili V. Kuznetsov
(Head of Delegation)

Grigory I. Tunkin

Alternate Representatives

Alexander A. Afanasiev

Vice Admiral Valentin A. Chekurov

Mikhail M. Somov

Mikhail N. Smirnovsky

United Kingdom of Great Britain and Northern Ireland

Representatives

Sir Esler Dening, G.C.M.G., O.B.E.
(Head of Delegation)

His Excellency
Sir Harold Caccia, G.C.M.G., K.C.V.O.

Alternate Representatives

H. N. Brain, C.M.G., O.B.E.

The Viscount Hood, C.M.G.

The Honorable

United States of America

<u>Representative</u>

> The Honorable
> Herman Phleger
> (Head of Delegation)

<u>Alternate Representatives</u>

> The Honorable
> Paul C. Daniels
>
> George H. Owen

The Conference met at Washington on October 15, 1959. It had before it as a basis for discussion working papers considered in the course of informal preparatory talks among representatives of the twelve countries who had met in Washington following the aforesaid invitation of the Government of the United States of America.

At the opening Plenary Session of the Conference the Honorable Herman Phleger, Head of the United States Delegation, was elected Chairman of the Conference. Mr. Henry E. Allen was appointed Secretary General of the Conference and Rapporteur.

The Conference established two Committees under rotating chairmanship to deal with the items on the agenda of the Conference. Following initial consideration of such items, these Committees were reconstituted as a Committee of the Whole. There were also established a Credentials Committee, a Drafting Committee, and a Committee on Style.

The final session of the Conference was held on December 1, 1959.

As a result of the deliberations of the Conference, as recorded in the summary records and reports of the respective Committees and of the Plenary Sessions, the Conference formulated and submitted for signature on December 1, 1959, the Antarctic Treaty.

The Conference recommended to the participating Governments that they appoint representatives to meet in Washington within two months after the signing of the Treaty and thereafter at such times as may be convenient, pending the entry into force of the Treaty, to consult together and to recommend to their Governments such interim arrangements regarding the matters dealt with in the Treaty as they may deem desirable.

IN WITNESS WHEREOF, the following Plenipotentiaries sign this Final Act.

DONE at Washington this first day of December, one thousand nine hundred and fifty-nine, in the English, French, Russian and Spanish languages, each version being equally authentic, in a single original which shall be deposited in the archives of the Government of the United States of America. The Government of the United States of America shall transmit certified copies thereof to all the other Governments represented at the Conference.

FOR ARGENTINA:
POUR L'ARGENTINE:
ЗА АРГЕНТИНУ:
POR LA ARGENTINA:

FOR AUSTRALIA:
POUR L'AUSTRALIE:
ЗА АВСТРАЛИЮ:
POR AUSTRALIA:

FOR BELGIUM:
POUR LA BELGIQUE:
ЗА БЕЛЬГИЮ:
POR BELGICA:

FOR CHILE:
POUR LE CHILI:
ЗА ЧИЛИ:
POR CHILE:

FOR THE FRENCH REPUBLIC:
POUR LA REPUBLIQUE FRANCAISE:
ЗА ФРАНЦУЗСКУЮ РЕСПУБЛИКУ:
POR LA REPUBLICA FRANCESA:

FOR JAPAN:
POUR LE JAPON:
ЗА ЯПОНИЮ:
POR JAPON:

FOR NEW ZEALAND
POUR LA NOUVELLE-ZELANDE:
ЗА НОВУЮ ЗЕЛАНДИЮ:
POR NUEVA ZELANDIA:

FOR NORWAY
POUR LA NORVEGE:
ЗА НОРВЕГИЮ:
POR NORUEGA:

FOR THE UNION OF SOUTH AFRICA:
POUR L'UNION SUD-AFRICAINE:
ЗА ЮЖНО-АФРИКАНСКИЙ СОЮЗ:
POR LA UNION DEL AFRICA DEL SUR:

FOR THE UNION OF SOVIET SOCIALIST REPUBLICS:
POUR L'UNION DES REPUBLIQUES SOCIALISTES SOVIETIQUES:
ЗА СОЮЗ СОВЕТСКИХ СОЦИАЛИСТИЧЕСКИХ РЕСПУБЛИК:
POR LA UNION DE REPUBLICAS SOCIALISTAS SOVIETICAS:

FOR THE UNITED KINGDOM OF GREAT BRITAIN AND NORTHERN IRELAND:
POUR LE ROYAUME-UNI DE GRANDE-BRETAGNE ET D'IRLANDE DU NORD:
ЗА СОЕДИНЕННОЕ КОРОЛЕВСТВО ВЕЛИКОБРИТАНИИ И СЕВЕРНОЙ ИРЛАНДИИ:
POR EL REINO UNIDO DE GRAN BRETANA E IRLANDA DEL NORTE:

FOR THE UNITED STATES OF AMERICA:
POUR LES ETATS-UNIS D'AMERIQUE:
ЗА СОЕДИНЕННЫЕ ШТАТЫ АМЕРИКИ:
POR LOS ESTADOS UNIDOS DE AMERICA:

I CERTIFY THAT the foregoing is a true copy of the Final Act of the Conference on Antarctica signed at Washington on December 1, 1959 in the English, French, Russian, and Spanish languages, the signed original of which is deposited in the archives of the Government of the United States of America.

IN TESTIMONY WHEREOF, I, CHRISTIAN A. HERTER, Secretary of State of the United States of America, have hereunto caused the seal of the Department of State to be affixed and my name subscribed by the Authentication Officer of the said Department, at the city of Washington, in the District of Columbia, this second day of December, 1959.

____
Secretary of State

By _______________________________
Authentication Officer
Department of State

THE ANTARCTIC TREATY

The Governments of Argentina, Australia, Belgium, Chile, the French Republic, Japan, New Zealand, Norway, the Union of South Africa, the Union of Soviet Socialist Republics, the United Kingdom of Great Britain and Northern Ireland, and the United States of America,

Recognizing that it is in the interest of all mankind that Antarctica shall continue for ever to be used exclusively for peaceful purposes and shall not become the scene or object of international discord;

Acknowledging the substantial contributions to scientific knowledge resulting from international cooperation in scientific investigation in Antarctica;

Convinced that the establishment of a firm foundation for the continuation and development of such cooperation on the basis of freedom of scientific investigation in Antarctica as applied during the International Geophysical Year accords with the interests of science and the progress of all mankind;

Convinced also that a treaty ensuring the use of Antarctica for peaceful purposes only and the continuance of international harmony in Antarctica will further the purposes and principles embodied in the Charter of the United Nations;

Have agreed as follows:

ARTICLE I

1.   Antarctica shall be used for peaceful purposes only. There shall be prohibited, *inter alia*, any measures of a military nature, such as the establishment of military bases and fortifications, the carrying out of military maneuvers, as well as the testing of any type of weapons.

2.   The present Treaty shall not prevent the use of military personnel or equipment for scientific research or for any other peaceful purpose.

ARTICLE II

Freedom of scientific investigation in Antarctica and cooperation toward that end, as applied during the International Geophysical Year, shall continue, subject to the provisions of the present Treaty.

ARTICLE III

1.   In order to promote international cooperation in scientific investigation in Antarctica, as provided for in Article II of the present Treaty, the Contracting Parties agree that, to the greatest extent feasible and practicable:

> (a)   information regarding plans for scientific programs in Antarctica shall be exchanged to permit maximum economy and efficiency of operations;
>
> (b)   scientific personnel shall be exchanged in Antarctica between expeditions and stations;
>
> (c)   scientific observations and results from Antarctica shall be exchanged and made freely available.

2.   In implementing this Article, every encouragement shall be given to the establishment of cooperative working relations with those Specialized Agencies of the United Nations and other international organizations having a scientific or technical interest in Antarctica.

ARTICLE IV

1.   Nothing contained in the present Treaty shall be interpreted as:

> (a)   a renunciation by any Contracting Party of previously asserted rights of or claims to territorial sovereignty in Antarctica;
>
> (b)   a renunciation or diminution by any Contracting Party of any basis of claim to territorial sovereignty in Antarctica which it may have whether as a result of its activities or those of its nationals in Antarctica, or otherwise;
>
> (c)   prejudicing the position of any Contracting Party as regards its recognition or non-recognition of any other State's right of or claim or basis of claim to territorial sovereignty in Antarctica.

2.   No acts or activities taking place while the present Treaty is in force shall constitute a basis for asserting, supporting or denying a claim to territorial sovereignty in Antarctica or create any rights of sovereignty in Antarctica. No new claim, or enlargement of an existing claim, to territorial sovereignty in Antarctica shall be asserted while the present Treaty is in force.

ARTICLE V

1.   Any nuclear explosions in Antarctica and the disposal there of radioactive waste material shall be prohibited.

2. In the event of the conclusion of international agreements concerning the use of nuclear energy, including nuclear explosions and the disposal of radioactive waste material, to which all of the Contracting Parties whose representatives are entitled to participate in the meetings provided for under Article IX are parties, the rules established under such agreements shall apply in Antarctica.

ARTICLE VI

The provisions of the present Treaty shall apply to the area south of 60° South Latitude, including all ice shelves, but nothing in the present Treaty shall prejudice or in any way affect the rights, or the exercise of the rights, of any State under international law with regard to the high seas within that area.

ARTICLE VII

1. In order to promote the objectives and ensure the observance of the provisions of the present Treaty, each Contracting Party whose representatives are entitled to participate in the meetings referred to in Article IX of the Treaty shall have the right to designate observers to carry out any inspection provided for by the present Article. Observers shall be nationals of the Contracting Parties which designate them. The names of observers shall be communicated to every other Contracting Party having the right to designate observers, and like notice shall be given of the termination of their appointment.

2. Each observer designated in accordance with the provisions of paragraph 1 of this Article shall have complete freedom of access at any time to any or all areas of Antarctica.

3. All areas of Antarctica, including all stations, installations and equipment within those areas, and all ships and aircraft at points of discharging or embarking cargoes or personnel in Antarctica, shall be open at all times to inspection by any observers designated in accordance with paragraph 1 of this Article.

4. Aerial observation may be carried out at any time over any or all areas of Antarctica by any of the Contracting Parties having the right to designate observers.

5. Each Contracting Party shall, at the time when the present Treaty enters into force for it, inform the other Contracting Parties, and thereafter shall give them notice in advance, of

    (a) all expeditions to and within Antarctica, on the part of its ships or nationals, and all expeditions to Antarctica organized in or proceeding from its territory;

(b)   all stations in Antarctica occupied by its nationals; and

(c)   any military personnel or equipment intended to be introduced by it into Antarctica subject to the conditions prescribed in paragraph 2 of Article I of the present Treaty.

ARTICLE VIII

1.   In order to facilitate the exercise of their functions under the present Treaty, and without prejudice to the respective positions of the Contracting Parties relating to jurisdiction over all other persons in Antarctica, observers designated under paragraph 1 of Article VII and scientific personnel exchanged under subparagraph 1(b) of Article III of the Treaty, and members of the staffs accompanying any such persons, shall be subject only to the jurisdiction of the Contracting Party of which they are nationals in respect of all acts or omissions occurring while they are in Antarctica for the purpose of exercising their functions.

2.   Without prejudice to the provisions of paragraph 1 of this Article, and pending the adoption of measures in pursuance of subparagraph 1(e) of Article IX, the Contracting Parties concerned in any case of dispute with regard to the exercise of jurisdiction in Antarctica shall immediately consult together with a view to reaching a mutually acceptable solution.

ARTICLE IX

1.   Representatives of the Contracting Parties named in the preamble to the present Treaty shall meet at the City of Canberra within two months after the date of entry into force of the Treaty, and thereafter at suitable intervals and places, for the purpose of exchanging information, consulting together on matters of common interest pertaining to Antarctica, and formulating and considering, and recommending to their Governments, measures in furtherance of the principles and objectives of the Treaty, including measures regarding:

(a)   use of Antarctica for peaceful purposes only;

(b)   facilitation of scientific research in Antarctica;

(c)   facilitation of international scientific cooperation in Antarctica;

(d)   facilitation of the exercise of the rights of inspection provided for in Article VII of the Treaty;

(e)   questions relating to the exercise of jurisdiction in Antarctica;

(f)   preservation and conservation of living resources in Antarctica.

2.   Each Contracting Party which has become a party to the present Treaty by accession under Article XIII shall be entitled to appoint representatives to participate in the meetings referred to in paragraph 1 of the present Article, during such time as that Contracting Party demonstrates its interest in Antarctica by conducting substantial scientific research activity there, such as the establishment of a scientific station or the despatch of a scientific expedition.

3.   Reports from the observers referred to in Article VII of the present Treaty shall be transmitted to the representatives of the Contracting Parties participating in the meetings referred to in paragraph 1 of the present Article.

4.   The measures referred to in paragraph 1 of this Article shall become effective when approved by all the Contracting Parties whose representatives were entitled to participate in the meetings held to consider those measures.

5.   Any or all of the rights established in the present Treaty may be exercised as from the date of entry into force of the Treaty whether or not any measures facilitating the exercise of such rights have been proposed, considered or approved as provided in this Article.

ARTICLE X

Each of the Contracting Parties undertakes to exert appropriate efforts, consistent with the Charter of the United Nations, to the end that no one engages in any activity in Antarctica contrary to the principles or purposes of the present Treaty.

ARTICLE XI

1.   If any dispute arises between two or more of the Contracting Parties concerning the interpretation or application of the present Treaty, those Contracting Parties shall consult among themselves with a view to having the dispute resolved by negotiation, inquiry, mediation, conciliation, arbitration, judicial settlement or other peaceful means of their own choice.

2.   Any dispute of this character not so resolved shall, with the consent, in each case, of all parties to the dispute, be referred to the International Court of Justice for settlement; but failure to reach agreement on reference to the International Court shall not absolve parties to the dispute from the responsibility of continuing to seek to resolve it by any of the various peaceful means referred to in paragraph 1 of this Article.

ARTICLE XII

1. (a) The present Treaty may be modified or amended at any time by unanimous agreement of the Contracting Parties whose representatives are entitled to participate in the meetings provided for under Article IX. Any such modification or amendment shall enter into force when the depositary Government has received notice from all such Contracting Parties that they have ratified it.

   (b) Such modification or amendment shall thereafter enter into force as to any other Contracting Party when notice of ratification by it has been received by the depositary Government. Any such Contracting Party from which no notice of ratification is received within a period of two years from the date of entry into force of the modification or amendment in accordance with the provisions of subparagraph 1(a) of this Article shall be deemed to have withdrawn from the present Treaty on the date of the expiration of such period.

2. (a) If after the expiration of thirty years from the date of entry into force of the present Treaty, any of the Contracting Parties whose representatives are entitled to participate in the meetings provided for under Article IX so requests by a communication addressed to the depositary Government, a Conference of all the Contracting Parties shall be held as soon as practicable to review the operation of the Treaty.

   (b) Any modification or amendment to the present Treaty which is approved at such a Conference by a majority of the Contracting Parties there represented, including a majority of those whose representatives are entitled to participate in the meetings provided for under Article IX, shall be communicated by the depositary Government to all the Contracting Parties immediately after the termination of the Conference and shall enter into force in accordance with the provisions of paragraph 1 of the present Article.

   (c) If any such modification or amendment has not entered into force in accordance with the provisions of subparagraph 1(a) of this Article within a period of two years after the date of its communication to all the Contracting Parties, any Contracting Party may at any time after the expiration of that period give notice to the depositary Government of its withdrawal from the present Treaty; and such withdrawal shall take effect two years after the receipt of the notice by the depositary Government.

ARTICLE XIII

1.   The present Treaty shall be subject to ratification by the signatory States. It shall be open for accession by any State which is a Member of the United Nations, or by any other State which may be invited to accede to the Treaty with the consent of all the Contracting Parties whose representatives are entitled to participate in the meetings provided for under Article IX of the Treaty.

2.   Ratification of or accession to the present Treaty shall be effected by each State in accordance with its constitutional processes.

3.   Instruments of ratification and instruments of accession shall be deposited with the Government of the United States of America, hereby designated as the depositary Government.

4.   The depositary Government shall inform all signatory and acceding States of the date of each deposit of an instrument of ratification or accession, and the date of entry into force of the Treaty and of any modification or amendment thereto.

5.   Upon the deposit of instruments of ratification by all the signatory States, the present Treaty shall enter into force for those States and for States which have deposited instruments of accession. Thereafter the Treaty shall enter into force for any acceding State upon the deposit of its instrument of accession.

6.   The present Treaty shall be registered by the depositary Government pursuant to Article 102 of the Charter of the United Nations.

ARTICLE XIV

The present Treaty, done in the English, French, Russian and Spanish languages, each version being equally authentic, shall be deposited in the archives of the Government of the United States of America, which shall transmit duly certified copies thereof to the Governments of the signatory and acceding States.

ENVIRONMENT PROTOCOL

FINAL ACT OF THE ELEVENTH ANTARCTIC TREATY SPECIAL CONSULTATIVE MEETING

The final session of the XIth Antarctic Treaty Special Consultative Meeting, convened in accordance with the Recommendation XV-I, was held at Madrid on the 3rd and 4th of October, 1991. The Meeting was attended by representatives of the Antarctic Treaty Consultative Parties (Argentina, Australia, Belgium, Brazil, Chile, China, Ecuador, Finland, France, Germany, India, Italy, Japan, The Netherlands, New Zealand, Norway, Peru, Poland, the Republic of Korea, South Africa, Spain, Sweden, the Union of Soviet Socialist Republics, the United Kingdom, the United States of America and Uruguay). The Meeting was also attended by delegations from Contracting Parties to the Antarctic Treaty which are not Consultative Parties (Austria, Bulgaria, Canada, Colombia, Cuba, Czechoslovakia, Denmark, Greece, Hungary, the Democratic People's Republic of Korea, Romania and Switzerland). Representatives of international governmental and non-governmental organisations attended the Meeting as observers (Antarctic and Southern Ocean Coalition, Scientific Committee on Antarctic Research, Commission for the Conservation of Antarctic Marine Living Resources, Commission of the European Communities, Intergovernmental Oceanographic Commission, World Meteorological Organisation, International Union for the Conservation of Nature and Natural Resources).

As a result of the deliberations, summarised in the Final Report of the XIth Antarctic Treaty Special Consultative Meeting, the Antarctic Treaty Consultative Parties adopted in the official languages of the Antarctic Treaty the "Protocol on Environmental Protection to the Antarctic Treaty" and four Annexes to the Protocol, which form an integral part thereof, namely: Annex I on Environmental Impact Assessment, Annex II on Conservation of Antarctic Fauna and Flora, Annex III on Waste Disposal and Waste Management, Annex IV on Prevention of Marine Pollution. The text of the Protocol and the four Annexes is attached to this Final Act. The Protocol provides for the possibility of adopting additional Annexes.

The Protocol provides that it will be opened for signature in Madrid on the 4th of October, 1991, and thereafter in Washington D.C. until the 3rd of October, 1992.

In the Protocol the Parties commit themselves to the comprehensive protection of the Antarctic environment and dependent and associated ecosystems, and designate Antarctica as a natural reserve devoted to peace and science.

In this context, the Meeting agreed that, pending entry into force of the protocol, which would take place as soon as possible, current constraints on Antarctic mineral resource activity should continue.

The Meeting noted that the harvesting of ice was not considered to be an Antarctic mineral resource activity; it was therefore agreed that if the harvesting of ice were to become possible in the future, it was understood that the provisions of the Protocol, other than Article 7, would apply.

The meeting noted that nothing in the Protocol shall derogate from the rights and obligations of Parties under the Convention on the Conservation of Antarctic Marine Living Resources, the Convention for the Conservation of Antarctic Seals and the International Convention for the Regulation of Whaling.

With respect to the activities referred to in Article 8, the Meeting noted that it was not intended that those activities should include activities undertaken in the Antarctic Treaty area pursuant to the Convention on the Conservation of Antarctic Marine Living Resources or the Convention for the Conservation of Antarctic Seals.

The Meeting underlined the commitment of the Parties to the Protocol in its Article 16 to elaborate rules and procedures relating to liability for damage arising from activities taking place in the Antarctic Treaty area and covered by the Protocol, with a view to their inclusion in one or more Annexes and expressed the wish that work on their elaboration could begin at an early stage. In this context, it was understood that liability for damage to the Antarctic environment should be included in such an elaboration.

The Meeting noted that, with regard to the competence of the Arbitral Tribunal under Articles 19 and 20 of the Protocol to make an award upon any matter, it was understood that the Tribunal would not make determinations as to damages until a binding legal regime had entered into force through an Annex or Annexes pursuant to Article 16.

With reference to Article 18, the Meeting agreed that an inquiry procedure should be elaborated to facilitate resolution of disputes concerning the interpretation or application of Article 3 with respect to activities undertaken or proposed to be undertaken in the Antarctic Treaty area.

The Meeting acknowledged that, while reservations to the Protocol would not be permitted, this did not preclude a State, when signing, ratifying, accepting or approving the Protocol, or when acceding to it, from making declarations or statements, however, phrased or named, with a view, *inter alia*, to the harmonisation of its laws and regulations with the Protocol, provided that such declarations or statements do not purport to exclude or to modify the legal effect of the Protocol in its application to that State.

The Meeting agreed that the contents of this Final Act are without prejudice to the legal position of any Party under Article IV of the Antarctic Treaty.

The Meeting agreed that it was desirable to ensure the effective implementation at an early date of the provisions of the Protocol. Pending the entry into force of the Protocol it was agreed that it was desirable for all Contracting Parties to the Antarctic Treaty to apply Annexes I-IV, in accordance with their legal systems and to the extent practicable, and to take individually such steps to enable it to occur as soon as possible.

Done in Madrid, this fourth day of October, 1991, in a single original copy in the four languages of the Antarctic Treaty to be deposited in the Archives of the Government of the United States of America, which will transmit a certified copy thereof to all Contracting Parties to the Antarctic Treaty.

PROTOCOL ON ENVIRONMENTAL PROTECTION TO THE ANTARCTIC TREATY

PREAMBLE

The States Parties to this Protocol to the Antarctic Treaty, hereinafter referred to as the Parties,

Convinced of the need to enhance the protection of the Antarctic environment and dependent and associated ecosystems;

Convinced of the need to strengthen the Antarctic Treaty system so as to ensure that Antarctica shall continue forever to be used exclusively for peaceful purposes and shall not become the scene or object of international discord;

Bearing in mind the special legal and political status of Antarctica and the special responsibility of the Antarctic Treaty Consultative Parties to ensure that all activities in Antarctica are consistent with the purposes and principles of the Antarctic Treaty;

Recalling the designation of Antarctica as a Special Conservation Area and other measures adopted under the Antarctic Treaty system to protect the Antarctic environment and dependent and associated ecosystems;

Acknowledging further the unique opportunities Antarctica offers for scientific monitoring of and research on processes of global as well as regional importance;

Reaffirming the conservation principles of the Convention on the Conservation of Antarctic Marine Living Resources;

Convinced that the development of a comprehensive regime for the protection of the Antarctic environment and dependent and associated ecosystems is in the interest of mankind as a whole;

Desiring to supplement the Antarctic Treaty to this end;

Have agreed as follows:

ARTICLE 1
DEFINITIONS

For the purposes of this Protocol:

(a)   "The Antarctic Treaty" means the Antarctic Treaty done at Washington on 1 December 1959;

(b)   "Antarctic Treaty area" means the area to which the provisions of the Antarctic Treaty apply in accordance with Article VI of that Treaty;

(c)   "Antarctic Treaty Consultative Meetings" means the meetings referred to in Article IX of the Antarctic Treaty;

(d)   "Antarctic Treaty Consultative Parties" means the Contracting Parties to the Antarctic Treaty entitled to appoint representatives to participate in the meetings referred to in Article IX of that Treaty;

(e)   "Antarctic Treaty system" means the Antarctic Treaty, the measures in effect under that Treaty, its associated separate international instruments in force and the measures in effect under those instruments;

(f)   "Arbitral Tribunal" means the Arbitral Tribunal established in accordance with the Schedule to this Protocol, which forms an integral part thereof;

(g)   "Committee" means the Committee for Environmental Protection established in accordance with Article 11.

ARTICLE 2
Objective and Designation

The Parties commit themselves to the comprehensive protection of the Antarctic environment and dependent and associated ecosystems and hereby designate Antarctica as a natural reserve, devoted to peace and science.

ARTICLE 3
Environmental Principles

1.   The protection of the Antarctic environment and dependent and associated ecosystems and the intrinsic value of Antarctica, including its wilderness and aesthetic values and its value as an area for the conduct of scientific research, in particular research essential to understanding the global environment, shall be fundamental considerations in the planning and conduct of all activities in the Antarctic Treaty area.

2.   To this end:

(a)   activities in the Antarctic Treaty area shall be planned and conducted so as to limit adverse impacts on the Antarctic environment and dependent and associated ecosystems;

(b)   activities in the Antarctic Treaty area shall be planned and conducted so as to avoid:

  (i)   adverse effects on climate or weather patterns;

  (ii)   significant adverse effects on air or water quality;

  (iii)   significant changes in the atmospheric, terrestrial (including aquatic), glacial or marine environments;

  (iv)   detrimental changes in the distribution, abundance or productivity of species or populations of species of fauna and flora;

  (v)   further jeopardy to endangered or threatened species or populations of such species; or

  (vi)   degradation of, or substantial risk to, areas of biological, scientific, historic, aesthetic or wilderness significance;

(c)   activities in the Antarctic Treaty area shall be planned and conducted on the basis of information sufficient to allow prior assessments of, and informed judgments about, their possible impacts on the Antarctic environment and dependent and associated ecosystems and on the value of Antarctica for the conduct of scientific research; such judgments shall take account of:

  (i)   the scope of the activity, including its area, duration and intensity;

  (ii)   the cumulative impacts of the activity, both by itself and in combination with other activities in the Antarctic Treaty area;

  (iii)   whether the activity will detrimentally affect any other activity in the Antarctic Treaty area;

  (iv)   whether technology and procedures are available to provide for environmentally safe operations;

  (v)   whether there exists the capacity to monitor key environmental parameters and ecosystem components so as to identify and provide early warning of any adverse effects of the activity and to provide for such modification of operating procedures as may be necessary in the light of the results of monitoring or increased knowledge of the Antarctic environment and dependent and associated ecosystems; and

  (vi)   whether there exists the capacity to respond promptly and effectively to accidents, particularly those with potential environmental effects;

(d)   regular and effective monitoring shall take place to allow assessment of the impacts of ongoing activities, including the verification of predicted impacts;

(e)   regular and effective monitoring shall take place to facilitate early detection of the possible unforeseen effects of activities carried on both within and outside the Antarctic Treaty area on the Antarctic environment and dependent and associated ecosystems.

3.   Activities shall be planned and conducted in the Antarctic Treaty area so as to accord priority to scientific research and to preserve the value of Antarctica as an area for the conduct of such research, including research essential to understanding the global environment.

4.   Activities undertaken in the Antarctic Treaty area pursuant to scientific research programmes, tourism and all other governmental and non-governmental activities in the Antarctic Treaty area for which advance notice is required in accordance with Article VII (5) of the Antarctic Treaty, including associated logistic support activities, shall:

(a)   take place in a manner consistent with the principles in this Article; and

(b)   be modified, suspended or cancelled if they result in or threaten to result in impacts upon the Antarctic environment or dependent or associated ecosystems inconsistent with those principles.

ARTICLE 4

RELATIONSHIP WITH THE OTHER COMPONENTS OF THE ANTARCTIC TREATY SYSTEM

1.   This Protocol shall supplement the Antarctic Treaty and shall neither modify nor amend that Treaty.

2.   Nothing in this Protocol shall derogate from the rights and obligations of the Parties to this Protocol under the other international instruments in force within the Antarctic Treaty system.

ARTICLE 5

CONSISTENCY WITH THE OTHER COMPONENTS OF THE ANTARCTIC TREATY SYSTEM

The Parties shall consult and co-operate with the Contracting Parties to the other international instruments in force within the Antarctic Treaty system and their respective institutions with a view to ensuring the achievement of the objectives and principles of this Protocol and avoiding any interference with the achievement of the objectives and principles of those instruments or any inconsistency between the implementation of those instruments and of this Protocol.

ARTICLE 6

CO-OPERATION

1.   The Parties shall co-operate in the planning and conduct of activities in the Antarctic Treaty area. To this end, each Party shall endeavour to:

    (a)   promote co-operative programmes of scientific, technical and educational value, concerning the protection of the Antarctic environment and dependent and associated ecosystems;

    (b)   provide appropriate assistance to other Parties in the preparation of environmental impact assessments;

    (c)   provide to other Parties upon request information relevant to any potential environmental risk and assistance to minimize the effects of accidents which may damage the Antarctic environment or dependent and associated ecosystems;

    (d)   consult with other Parties with regard to the choice of sites for prospective stations and other facilities so as to avoid the cumulative impacts caused by their excessive concentration in any location;

    (e)   where appropriate, undertake joint expeditions and share the use of stations and other facilities; and

    (f)   carry out such steps as may be agreed upon at Antarctic Treaty Consultative Meetings.

2.   Each Party undertakes, to the extent possible, to share information that may be helpful to other Parties in planning and conducting their activities in the Antarctic Treaty area, with a view to the protection of the Antarctic environment and dependent and associated ecosystems.

3.   The Parties shall co-operate with those Parties which may exercise jurisdiction in areas adjacent to the Antarctic Treaty area with a view to ensuring that activities in the Antarctic Treaty area do not have adverse environmental impacts on those areas.

ARTICLE 7

PROHIBITION OF MINERAL RESOURCE ACTIVITIES

Any activity relating to mineral resources, other than scientific research, shall be prohibited.

ARTICLE 8

ENVIRONMENTAL IMPACT ASSESSMENT

1.   Proposed activities referred to in paragraph 2 below shall be subject to the procedures set out in Annex I for prior assessment of the impacts of those activities on the Antarctic environment or on dependent or associated ecosystems according to whether those activities are identified as having:

     (a)   less than a minor or transitory impact;

     (b)   a minor or transitory impact; or

     (c)   more than a minor or transitory impact.

2.   Each Party shall ensure that the assessment procedures set out in Annex I are applied in the planning processes leading to decisions about any activities undertaken in the Antarctic Treaty area pursuant to scientific research programmes, tourism and all other governmental and non-governmental activities in the Antarctic Treaty area for which advance notice is required under Article VII (5) of the Antarctic Treaty, including associated logistic support activities.

3.   The assessment procedures set out in Annex I shall apply to any change in an activity whether the change arises from an increase or decrease in the intensity of an existing activity, from the addition of an activity, the decommissioning of a facility, or otherwise.

4.   Where activities are planned jointly by more than one Party, the Parties involved shall nominate one of their number to coordinate the implementation of the environmental impact assessment procedures set out in Annex I.

ARTICLE 9

ANNEXES

1.   The Annexes to this Protocol shall form an integral part thereof.

2.   Annexes, additional to Annexes I-IV, may be adopted and become effective in accordance with Article IX of the Antarctic Treaty.

3.   Amendments and modifications to Annexes may be adopted and become effective in accordance with Article IX of the Antarctic Treaty, provided that any Annex may itself make provision for amendments and modifications to become effective on an accelerated basis.

4.   Annexes and any amendments and modifications thereto which have become effective in accordance with paragraphs 2 and 3 above shall, unless an Annex itself provides otherwise in respect of the entry into effect of any amendment or modification thereto, become effective for a Contracting Party to the Antarctic

Treaty which is not an Antarctic Treaty Consultative Party, or which was not an Antarctic Treaty Consultative Party at the time of the adoption, when notice of approval of that Contracting Party has been received by the Depository.

5.   Annexes shall, except to the extent that an Annex provides otherwise, be subject to the procedures for dispute settlement set out in Articles 18 to 20.

ARTICLE 10
ANTARCTIC TREATY CONSULTATIVE MEETINGS

1.   Antarctic Treaty Consultative Meetings shall, drawing upon the best scientific and technical advice available:

> (a)   define, in accordance with the provisions of this Protocol, the general policy for the comprehensive protection of the Antarctic environment and dependent and associated ecosystems; and

> (b)   adopt measures under Article IX of the Antarctic Treaty for the implementation of this Protocol.

2.   Antarctic Treaty Consultative Meetings shall review the work of the Committee and shall draw fully upon its advice and recommendations in carrying out the tasks referred to in paragraph 1 above, as well as upon the advice of the Scientific Committee on Antarctic Research.

ARTICLE 11
COMMITTEE FOR ENVIRONMENTAL PROTECTION

1.   There is hereby established the Committee for Environmental Protection.

2.   Each Party shall be entitled to be a member of the Committee and to appoint a representative who may be accompanied by experts and advisers.

3.   Observer status in the Committee shall be open to any Contracting Party to the Antarctic Treaty which is not a Party to this Protocol.

4.   The Committee shall invite the President of the Scientific Committee on Antarctic Research and the Chairman of the Scientific Committee for the Conservation of Antarctic Marine Living Resources to participate as observers at its sessions. The Committee may also, with the approval of the Antarctic Treaty Consultative Meeting, invite such other relevant scientific, environmental and technical organisations which can contribute to its work to participate as observers at its sessions.

5.   The Committee shall present a report on each of its sessions to the Antarctic Treaty Consultative Meeting. The report shall cover all matters considered at the

session and shall reflect the views expressed. The report shall be circulated to the Parties and to observers attending the session, and shall thereupon be made publicly available.

6.   The Committee shall adopt its rules of procedure which shall be subject to approval by the Antarctic Treaty Consultative Meeting.

ARTICLE 12
FUNCTIONS OF THE COMMITTEE

1.   The functions of the Committee shall be to provide advice and formulate recommendations to the Parties in connection with the implementation of this Protocol, including the operation of its Annexes, for consideration at Antarctic Treaty Consultative Meetings, and to perform such other functions as may be referred to it by the Antarctic Treaty Consultative Meetings. In particular, it shall provide advice on:

(a)   the effectiveness of measures taken pursuant to this Protocol;

(b)   the need to update, strengthen or otherwise improve such measures;

(c)   the need for additional measures, including the need for additional Annexes, where appropriate;

(d)   the application and implementation of the environmental impact assessment procedures set out in Article 8 and Annex I;

(e)   means of minimising or mitigating environmental impacts of activities in the Antarctic Treaty area;

(f)   procedures for situations requiring urgent action, including response action in environmental emergencies;

(g)   the operation and further elaboration of the Antarctic Protected Area system;

(h)   inspection procedures, including formats for inspection reports and checklists for the conduct of inspections;

(i)   the collection, archiving, exchange and evaluation of information related to environmental protection;

(j)   the state of the Antarctic environment; and

(k)   the need for scientific research, including environmental monitoring, related to the implementation of this Protocol.

2.   In carrying out its functions, the Committee shall, as appropriate, consult with the Scientific Committee on Antarctic Research, the Scientific Committee for the Conservation of Antarctic Marine Living Resources and other relevant scientific, environmental and technical organizations.

ARTICLE 13
COMPLIANCE WITH THIS PROTOCOL

1.	Each Party shall take appropriate measures within its competence, including the adoption of laws and regulations, administrative actions and enforcement measures, to ensure compliance with this Protocol.

2.	Each Party shall exert appropriate efforts, consistent with the Charter of the United Nations, to the end that no one engages in any activity contrary to this Protocol.

3.	Each Party shall notify all other Parties of the measures it takes pursuant to paragraphs 1 and 2 above.

4.	Each Party shall draw the attention of all other Parties to any activity which in its opinion affects the implementation of the objectives and principles of this Protocol.

5.	The Antarctic Treaty Consultative Meetings shall draw the attention of any State which is not a Party to this Protocol to any activity undertaken by that State, its agencies, instrumentalities, natural or juridical persons, ships, aircraft or other means of transport which affects the implementation of the objectives and principles of this Protocol.

ARTICLE 14
INSPECTION

1.	In order to promote the protection of the Antarctic environment and dependent and associated ecosystems, and to ensure compliance with this Protocol, the Antarctic Treaty Consultative Parties shall arrange, individually or collectively, for inspections by observers to be made in accordance with Article VII of the Antarctic Treaty.

2.	Observers are:

(a)	observers designated by any Antarctic Treaty Consultative Party who shall be nationals of that Party; and

(b)	any observers designated at Antarctic Treaty Consultative Meetings to carry out inspections under procedures to be established by an Antarctic Treaty Consultative Meeting.

3.	Parties shall co-operate fully with observers undertaking inspections, and shall ensure that during inspections, observers are given access to all parts of stations, installations, equipment, ships and aircraft open to inspection under Article VII (3) of the Antarctic Treaty, as well as to all records maintained thereon which are called for pursuant to this Protocol.

4.   Reports of inspections shall be sent to the Parties whose stations, installations, equipment, ships or aircraft are covered by the reports. After those Parties have been given the opportunity to comment, the reports and any comments thereon shall be circulated to all the Parties and to the Committee, considered at the next Antarctic Treaty Consultative Meeting, and thereafter made publicly available.

ARTICLE 15
EMERGENCY RESPONSE ACTION

1.   In order to respond to environmental emergencies in the Antarctic Treaty area, each Party agrees to:

(a)   provide for prompt and effective response action to such emergencies which might arise in the performance of scientific research programmes, tourism and all other governmental and non-governmental activities in the Antarctic Treaty area for which advance notice is required under Article VII (5) of the Antarctic Treaty, including associated logistic support activities; and

(b)   establish contingency plans for response to incidents with potential adverse effects on the Antarctic environment or dependent and associated ecosystems.

2.   To this end, the Parties shall:

(a)   co-operate in the formulation and implementation of such contingency plans; and

(b)   establish procedures for immediate notification of, and co-operative response to, environmental emergencies.

3.   In the implementation of this Article, the Parties shall draw upon the advice of the appropriate international organisations.

ARTICLE 16
LIABILITY

Consistent with the objectives of this Protocol for the comprehensive protection of the Antarctic environment and dependent and associated ecosystems, the Parties undertake to elaborate rules and procedures relating to liability for damage arising from activities taking place in the Antarctic Treaty area and covered by this Protocol.

Those rules and procedures shall be included in one or more Annexes to be adopted in accordance with Article 9 (2).

ARTICLE 17
ANNUAL REPORT BY PARTIES

1.   Each Party shall report annually on the steps taken to implement this Protocol. Such reports shall include notifications made in accordance with Article 13 (3), contingency plans established in accordance with Article 15 and any other notifications and information called for pursuant to this Protocol for which there is no other provision concerning the circulation and exchange of information.

2.   Reports made in accordance with paragraph 1 above shall be circulated to all Parties and to the Committee, considered at the next Antarctic Treaty Consultative Meeting, and made publicly available.

ARTICLE 18
DISPUTE SETTLEMENT

If a dispute arises concerning the interpretation or application of this Protocol, the parties to the dispute shall, at the request of any one of them, consult among themselves as soon as possible with a view to having the dispute resolved by negotiation, inquiry, mediation, conciliation, arbitration, judicial settlement or other peaceful means to which the parties to the dispute agree.

ARTICLE 19
CHOICE OF DISPUTE SETTLEMENT PROCEDURE

1.   Each Party, when signing, ratifying, accepting, approving or acceding to this Protocol, or at any time thereafter, may choose, by written declaration, one or both of the following means for the settlement of disputes concerning the interpretation or application of Articles 7, 8 and 15 and, except to the extent that an Annex provides otherwise, the provisions of any Annex and, insofar as it relates to these Articles and provisions, Article 13:

    (a)   the International Court of Justice;

    (b)   the Arbitral Tribunal.

2.   A declaration made under paragraph 1 above shall not affect the operation of Article 18 and Article 20 (2).

3.   A Party which has not made a declaration under paragraph 1 above or in respect of which a declaration is no longer in force shall be deemed to have accepted the competence of the Arbitral Tribunal.

4.   If the parties to a dispute have accepted the same means for the settlement of a dispute, the dispute may be submitted only to that procedure, unless the parties otherwise agree.

5.   If the parties to a dispute have not accepted the same means for the settlement of a dispute, or if they have both accepted both means, the dispute may be submitted only to the Arbitral Tribunal, unless the parties otherwise agree.

6.   A declaration made under paragraph 1 above shall remain in force until it expires in accordance with its terms or until three months after written notice of revocation has been deposited with the Depositary.

7.   A new declaration, a notice of revocation or the expiry of a declaration shall not in any way affect proceedings pending before the International Court of Justice or the Arbitral Tribunal, unless the parties to the dispute otherwise agree.

8.   Declarations and notices referred to in this Article shall be deposited with the Depositary who shall transmit copies thereof to all Parties.

ARTICLE 20
DISPUTE SETTLEMENT PROCEDURE

1.   If the parties to a dispute concerning the interpretation or application of Articles 7, 8 or 15 or, except to the extent that an Annex provides otherwise, the provisions of any Annex or, insofar as it relates to these Articles and provisions, Article 13, have not agreed on a means for resolving it within 12 months of the request for consultation pursuant to Article 18, the dispute shall be referred, at the request of any party to the dispute, for settlement in accordance with the procedure determined by Article 19 (4) and (5).

2.   The Arbitral Tribunal shall not be competent to decide or rule upon any matter within the scope of Article IV of the Antarctic Treaty. In addition, nothing in this Protocol shall be interpreted as conferring competence or jurisdiction on the International Court of Justice or any other tribunal established for the purpose of settling disputes between Parties to decide or otherwise rule upon any matter within the scope of Article IV of the Antarctic Treaty.

ARTICLE 21

SIGNATURE

This Protocol shall be open for signature at Madrid on the 4th of October 1991 and thereafter at Washington until the 3rd of October 1992 by any State which is a Contracting Party to the Antarctic Treaty.

ARTICLE 22

RATIFICATION, ACCEPTANCE, APPROVAL OR ACCESSION

1.	This Protocol is subject to ratification, acceptance or approval by signatory States.

2.	After the 3rd of October 1992 this Protocol shall be open for accession by any State which is a Contracting Party to the Antarctic Treaty.

3.	Instruments of ratification, acceptance, approval or accession shall be deposited with the Government of the United States of America, hereby designated as the Depositary.

4.	After the date on which this Protocol has entered into force, the Antarctic Treaty Consultative Parties shall not act upon a notification regarding the entitlement of a Contracting Party to the Antarctic Treaty to appoint representatives to participate in Antarctic Treaty Consultative Meetings in accordance with Article IX (2) of the Antarctic Treaty unless that Contracting Party has first ratified, accepted, approved or acceded to this Protocol.

ARTICLE 23

ENTRY INTO FORCE

1.	This Protocol shall enter into force on the thirtieth day following the date of deposit of instruments of ratification, acceptance, approval or accession by all States which are Antarctic Treaty Consultative Parties at the date on which this Protocol is adopted.

2.	For each Contracting Party to the Antarctic Treaty which, subsequent to the date of entry into force of this Protocol, deposits an instrument of ratification, acceptance, approval or accession, this Protocol shall enter into force on the thirtieth day following such deposit.

ARTICLE 24
RESERVATIONS

Reservations to this Protocol shall not be permitted.

ARTICLE 25
MODIFICATION OR AMENDMENT

1.   Without prejudice to the provisions of Article 9, this Protocol may be modified or amended at any time in accordance with the procedures set forth in Article XII (1) (a) and (b) of the Antarctic Treaty.

2.   If, after the expiration of 50 years from the date of entry into force of this Protocol, any of the Antarctic Treaty Consultative Parties so requests by a communication addressed to the Depositary, a conference shall be held as soon as practicable to review the operation of this Protocol.

3.   A modification or amendment proposed at any Review Conference called pursuant to paragraph 2 above shall be adopted by a majority of the Parties, including 3/4 of the States which are Antarctic Treaty Consultative Parties at the time of adoption of this Protocol.

4.   A modification or amendment adopted pursuant to paragraph 3 above shall enter into force upon ratification, acceptance, approval or accession by 3/4 of the Antarctic Treaty Consultative Parties, including ratification, acceptance, approval or accession by all States which are Antarctic Treaty Consultative Parties at the time of adoption of this Protocol.

5.   (a) With respect to Article 7, the prohibition on Antarctic mineral resource activities contained therein shall continue unless there is in force a binding legal regime on Antarctic mineral resource activities that includes anagreed means for determining whether, and, if so, under which conditions, any such activities would be acceptable. This regime shall fully safeguard the interests of all States referred to in Article IV of the Antarctic Treaty and apply the principles thereof. Therefore, if a modification or amendment to Article 7 is proposed at a Review Conference referred to in paragraph 2 above, it shall include such a binding legal regime.

(b) If any such modification or amendment has not entered into force within 3 years of the date of its adoption, any Party may at any time thereafter notify to the Depositary of its withdrawal from this Protocol, and such withdrawal shall take effect 2 years after receipt of the notification by the Depositary.

ARTICLE 26

NOTIFICATIONS BY THE DEPOSITARY

The Depositary shall notify all Contracting Parties to the Antarctic Treaty of the following:

(a) signatures of this Protocol and the deposit of instruments of ratification, acceptance, approval or accession;

(b) the date of entry into force of this Protocol and any additional Annex thereto;

(c) the date of entry into force of any amendment or modification to this Protocol;

(d) the deposit of declarations and notices pursuant to Article 19; and

(e) any notification received pursuant to Article 25 (5) (b).

ARTICLE 27

AUTHENTIC TEXTS AND REGISTRATION WITH THE UNITED NATIONS

1. This Protocol, done in the English, French, Russian and Spanish languages, each version being equally authentic, shall be deposited in the archives of the Government of the United States of America, which shall transmit duly certified copies thereof to all Contracting Parties to the Antarctic Treaty.

2. This Protocol shall be registered by the Depositary pursuant to Article 102 of the Charter of the United Nations.

SCHEDULE TO THE PROTOCOL

ARBITRATION

ARTICLE 1

1.   The Arbitral Tribunal shall be constituted and shall function in accordance with the Protocol, including this Schedule.

2.   The Secretary referred to in this Schedule is the Secretary General of the Permanent Court of Arbitration.

ARTICLE 2

1.   Each Party shall be entitled to designate up to three Arbitrators, at least one of whom shall be designated within three months of the entry into force of the Protocol for that Party. Each Arbitrator shall be experienced in Antarctic affairs, have thorough knowledge of international law and enjoy the highest reputation for fairness, competence and integrity. The names of the persons so designated shall constitute the list of Arbitrators. Each Party shall at all times maintain the name of at least one Arbitrator on the list.

2.   Subject to paragraph 3 below, an Arbitrator designated by a Party shall remain on the list for a period of five years and shall be eligible for redesignation by that Party for additional five year periods.

3.   A Party which designated an Arbitrator may withdraw the name of that Arbitrator from the list. If an Arbitrator dies or if a Party for any reason withdraws from the list the name of an Arbitrator designated by it, the Party which designated the Arbitrator in question shall notify the Secretary promptly. An Arbitrator whose name is withdrawn from the list shall continue to serve on any Arbitral Tribunal to which that Arbitrator has been appointed until the completion of proceedings before the Arbitral Tribunal.

4.   The Secretary shall ensure that an up-to-date list is maintained of the Arbitrators designated pursuant to this Article.

ARTICLE 3

1.   The Arbitral Tribunal shall be composed of three Arbitrators who shall be appointed as follows:

(a)   The party to the dispute commencing the proceedings shall appoint one Arbitrator, who may be its national, from the list referred to in Article 2.

This appointment shall be included in the notification referred to in Article 4.

(b) Within 40 days of the receipt of that notification, the other party to the dispute shall appoint the second Arbitrator, who may be its national, from the list referred to in Article 2.

(c) Within 60 days of the appointment of the second Arbitrator, the parties to the dispute shall appoint by agreement the third Arbitrator from the list referred to in Article 2.

The third Arbitrator shall not be either a national of a party to the dispute, or a person designated for the list referred to in Article 2 by a party to the dispute, or of the same nationality as either of the first two Arbitrators. The third Arbitrator shall be the Chairperson of the Arbitral Tribunal.

(d) If the second Arbitrator has not been appointed within the prescribed period, or if the parties to the dispute have not reached agreement within the prescribed period on the appointment of the third Arbitrator, the Arbitrator or Arbitrators shall be appointed, at the request of any party to the dispute and within 30 days of the receipt of such request, by the President of the International Court of Justice from the list referred to in Article 2 and subject to the conditions prescribed in subparagraphs (b) and (c) above. In performing the functions accorded him or her in this subparagraph, the President of the Court shall consult the parties to the dispute.

(e) If the President of the International Court of Justice is unable to perform the functions accorded him or her in subparagraph (d) above or is a national of a party to the dispute, the functions shall be performed by the Vice-President of the Court, except that if the Vice-President is unable to perform the functions or is a national of a party to the dispute the functions shall be performed by the next most senior member of the Court who is available and is not a national of a party to the dispute.

2. Any vacancy shall be filled in the manner prescribed for the initial appointment.

3. In any dispute involving more than two Parties, those Parties having the same interest shall appoint one Arbitrator by agreement within the period specified in paragraph 1 (b) above.

ARTICLE 4

The party to the dispute commencing proceedings shall so notify the other party or parties to the dispute and the Secretary in writing. Such notification shall include a statement of the claim and the grounds on which it is based. The notification shall be transmitted by the Secretary to all Parties.

ARTICLE 5

1.   Unless the parties to the dispute agree otherwise, arbitration shall take place at The Hague, where the records of the Arbitral Tribunal shall be kept. The Arbitral Tribunal shall adopt its own rules of procedure. Such rules shall ensure that each party to the dispute has a full opportunity to be heard and to present its case and shall also ensure that the proceedings are conducted expeditiously.

2.   The Arbitral Tribunal may hear and decide counterclaims arising out of the dispute.

ARTICLE 6

1.   The Arbitral Tribunal, where it considers that *prima facie* it has jurisdiction under the Protocol, may:

(a)   at the request of any party to a dispute, indicate such provisional measures as it considers necessary to preserve the respective rights of the parties to the dispute;

(b)   prescribe any provisional measures which it considers appropriate under the circumstances to prevent serious harm to the Antarctic environment or dependent or associated ecosystems.

2.   The parties to the dispute shall comply promptly with any provisional measures prescribed under paragraph 1 (b) above pending an award under Article 10.

3.   Notwithstanding the time period in Article 20 of the Protocol, a party to a dispute may at any time, by notification to the other party or parties to the dispute and to the Secretary in accordance with Article 4, request that the Arbitral Tribunal be constituted as a matter of exceptional urgency to indicate or prescribe emergency provisional measures in accordance with this Article. In such case, the Arbitral Tribunal shall be constituted as soon as possible in accordance with Article 3, except that the time periods in Article 3 (1) (b), (c) and (d) shall be reduced to 14 days in each case. The Arbitral Tribunal shall decide upon the request for emergency provisional measures within two months of the appointment of its Chairperson.

4.   Following a decision by the Arbitral Tribunal upon a request for emergency provisional measures in accordance with paragraph 3 above, settlement of the dispute shall proceed in accordance with Articles 18, 19 and 20 of the Protocol.

ARTICLE 7

Any Party which believes it has a legal interest, whether general or individual, which may be substantially affected by the award of an Arbitral Tribunal, may, unless the Arbitral Tribunal decides otherwise, intervene in the proceedings.

ARTICLE 8

The parties to the dispute shall facilitate the work of the Arbitral Tribunal and, in particular, in accordance with their law and using all means at their disposal, shall provide it with all relevant documents and information, and enable it, when necessary, to call witnesses or experts and receive their evidence.

ARTICLE 9

If one of the parties to the dispute does not appear before the Arbitral Tribunal or fails to defend its case, any other party to the dispute may request the Arbitral Tribunal to continue the proceedings and make its award.

ARTICLE 10

1.   The Arbitral Tribunal shall, on the basis of the provisions of the Protocol and other applicable rules and principles of international law that are not incompatible with such provisions, decide such disputes as are submitted to it.

2.   The Arbitral Tribunal may decide, *ex aequo et bono*, a dispute submitted to it, if the parties to the dispute so agree.

ARTICLE 11

1.   Before making its award, the Arbitral Tribunal shall satisfy itself that it has competence in respect of the dispute and that the claim or counterclaim is well founded in fact and law.

2.   The award shall be accompanied by a statement of reasons for the decision and shall be communicated to the Secretary who shall transmit it to all Parties.

3.   The award shall be final and binding on the parties to the dispute and on any Party which intervened in the proceedings and shall be complied with without delay. The Arbitral Tribunal shall interpret the award at the request of a party to the dispute or of any intervening Party.

4.   The award shall have no binding force except in respect of that particular case.

5.   Unless the Arbitral Tribunal decides otherwise, the expenses of the Arbitral Tribunal, including the remuneration of the Arbitrators, shall be borne by the parties to the dispute in equal shares.

ARTICLE 12

All decisions of the Arbitral Tribunal, including those referred to in Articles 5, 6 and 11, shall be made by a majority of the Arbitrators who may not abstain from voting.

ARTICLE 13

1.   This Schedule may be amended or modified by a measure adopted in accordance with Article IX (1) of the Antarctic Treaty. Unless the measure specifies otherwise, the amendment or modification shall be deemed to have been approved, and shall become effective, one year after the close of the Antarctic Treaty Consultative Meeting at which it was adopted, unless one or more of the Antarctic Treaty Consultative Parties notifies the Depositary, within that time period, that it wishes an extension of that period or that it is unable to approve the measure.

2.   Any amendment or modification of this Schedule which becomes effective in accordance with paragraph 1 above shall thereafter become effective as to any other Party when notice of approval by it has been received by the Depositary.

ANNEX I TO THE PROTOCOL ON ENVIRONMENTAL PROTECTION TO THE ANTARCTIC TREATY

ENVIRONMENTAL IMPACT ASSESSMENT

ARTICLE 1
PRELIMINARY STAGE

1.   The environmental impacts of proposed activities referred to in Article 8 of the Protocol shall, before their commencement, be considered in accordance with appropriate national procedures.

2.   If an activity is determined as having less than a minor or transitory impact, the activity may proceed forthwith.

ARTICLE 2
INITIAL ENVIRONMENTAL EVALUATION

1.   Unless it has been determined that an activity will have less than a minor or transitory impact, or unless a Comprehensive Environmental Evaluation is being prepared in accordance with Article 3, an Initial Environmental Evaluation shall be prepared. It shall contain sufficient detail to assess whether a proposed activity may have more than a minor or transitory impact and shall include:

(a)   a description of the proposed activity, including its purpose, location, duration and intensity; and

(b)   consideration of alternatives to the proposed activity and any impacts that the activity may have, including consideration of cumulative impacts in the light of existing and known planned activities.

2.   If an Initial Environmental Evaluation indicates that a proposed activity is likely to have no more than a minor or transitory impact, the activity may proceed, provided that appropriate procedures, which may include monitoring, are put in place to assess and verify the impact of the activity.

ARTICLE 3
COMPREHENSIVE ENVIRONMENTAL EVALUATION

1.   If an Initial Environmental Evaluation indicates or if it is otherwise determined that a proposed activity is likely to have more than a minor or transitory impact, a Comprehensive Environmental Evaluation shall be prepared.

2. A Comprehensive Environmental Evaluation shall include:

(a) a description of the proposed activity including its purpose, location, duration and intensity, and possible alternatives to the activity, including the alternative of not proceeding, and the consequences of those alternatives;

(b) a description of the initial environmental reference state with which predicted changes are to be compared and a prediction of the future environmental reference state in the absence of the proposed activity;

(c) a description of the methods and data used to forecast the impacts of the proposed activity;

(d) estimation of the nature, extent, duration, and intensity of the likely direct impacts of the proposed activity;

(e) consideration of possible indirect or second order impacts of the proposed activity;

(f) consideration of cumulative impacts of the proposed activity in the light of existing activities and other known planned activities;

(g) identification of measures, including monitoring programmes, that could be taken to minimise or mitigate impacts of the proposed activity and to detect unforeseen impacts and that could provide early warning of any adverse effects of the activity as well as to deal promptly and effectively with accidents;

(h) identification of unavoidable impacts of the proposed activity;

(i) consideration of the effects of the proposed activity on the conduct of scientific research and on other existing uses and values;

(j) an identification of gaps in knowledge and uncertainties encountered in compiling the information required under this paragraph;

(k) a non-technical summary of the information provided under this paragraph; and

(l) the name and address of the person or organization which prepared the Comprehensive Environmental Evaluation and the address to which comments thereon should be directed.

3. The draft Comprehensive Environmental Evaluation shall be made publicly available and shall be circulated to all Parties, which shall also make it publicly available, for comment. A period of 90 days shall be allowed for the receipt of comments.

4. The draft Comprehensive Environmental Evaluation shall be forwarded to the Committee at the same time as it is circulated to the Parties, and at least 120 days before the next Antarctic Treaty Consultative Meeting, for consideration as appropriate.

5. No final decision shall be taken to proceed with the proposed activity in the Antarctic Treaty area unless there has been an opportunity for consideration of the draft Comprehensive Environmental Evaluation by the Antarctic Treaty Consultative Meeting on the advice of the Committee, provided that no decision to proceed with a proposed activity shall be delayed through the operation of this paragraph for longer than 15 months from the date of circulation of the draft Comprehensive Environmental Evaluation.

6. A final Comprehensive Environmental Evaluation shall address and shall include or summarise comments received on the draft Comprehensive Environmental Evaluation. The final Comprehensive Environmental Evaluation, notice of any decisions relating thereto, and any evaluation of the significance of the predicted impacts in relation to the advantages of the proposed activity, shall be circulated to all Parties, which shall also make them publicly available, at least 60 days before the commencement of the proposed activity in the Antarctic Treaty area.

ARTICLE 4

DECISIONS TO BE BASED ON COMPREHENSIVE ENVIRONMENTAL EVALUATIONS

Any decision on whether a proposed activity, to which Article 3 applies, should proceed, and, if so, whether in its original or in a modified form, shall be based on the Comprehensive Environmental Evaluation as well as other relevant considerations.

ARTICLE 5

MONITORING

1. Procedures shall be put in place, including appropriate monitoring of key environmental indicators, to assess and verify the impact of any activity that proceeds following the completion of a Comprehensive Environmental Evaluation.

2. The procedures referred to in paragraph 1 above and in Article 2 (2) shall be designed to provide a regular and verifiable record of the impacts of the activity in order, *inter alia*, to:

    (a) enable assessments to be made of the extent to which such impacts are consistent with the Protocol; and

    (b) provide information useful for minimising or mitigating impacts, and, where appropriate, information on the need for suspension, cancellation or modification of the activity.

ARTICLE 6

Circulation of Information

1.   The following information shall be circulated to the Parties, forwarded to the Committee and made publicly available:

(a)   a description of the procedures referred to in Article 1;

(b)   an annual list of any Initial Environmental Evaluations prepared in accordance with Article 2 and any decisions taken in consequence thereof;

(c)   significant information obtained, and any action taken in consequence thereof, from procedures put in place in accordance with Articles 2 (2) and 5; and

(d)   information referred to in Article 3 (6).

2.   Any Initial Environmental Evaluation prepared in accordance with Article 2 shall be made available on request.

ARTICLE 7

Cases of Emergency

1.   This Annex shall not apply in cases of emergency relating to the safety of human life or of ships, aircraft or equipment and facilities of high value, or the protection of the environment, which require an activity to be undertaken without completion of the procedures set out in this Annex.

2.   Notice of activities undertaken in cases of emergency, which would otherwise have required preparation of a Comprehensive Environmental Evaluation, shall be circulated immediately to all Parties and to the Committee and a full explanation of the activities carried out shall be provided within 90 days of those activities.

ARTICLE 8

Amendment or Modification

1.   This Annex may be amended or modified by a measure adopted in accordance with Article IX (1) of the Antarctic Treaty. Unless the measure specifies otherwise, the amendment or modification shall be deemed to have been approved, and shall become effective, one year after the close of the Antarctic Treaty Consultative Meeting at which it was adopted, unless one or more of the Antarctic Treaty Consultative Parties notifies the Depositary, within that period, that it wishes an extension of that period or that it is unable to approve the measure.

2.	Any amendment or modification of this Annex which becomes effective in accordance with paragraph 1 above shall thereafter become effective as to any other Party when notice of approval by it has been received by the Depositary.

ANNEX II TO THE PROTOCOL ON ENVIRONMENTAL PROTECTION TO THE ANTARCTIC TREATY

CONSERVATION OF ANTARCTIC FAUNA AND FLORA

ARTICLE 1
DEFINITIONS

For the purposes of this Annex:

(a) "native mammal" means any member of any species belonging to the Class Mammalia, indigenous to the Antarctic Treaty area or occurring there naturally through migrations;

(b) "native bird" means any member, at any stage of its life cycle (including eggs), of any species of the Class Aves indigenous to the Antarctic Treaty area or occurring there naturally through migrations;

(c) "native plant" means any member of any species of terrestrial or freshwater vegetation, including bryophytes, lichens, fungi and algae, at any stage of its life cycle (including seeds, and other propagules), indigenous to the Antarctic Treaty area;

(d) "native invertebrate" means any member of any species of terrestrial or freshwater invertebrate, at any stage of its life cycle, indigenous to the Antarctic Treaty area;

(e) "appropriate authority" means any person or agency authorised by a Party to issue permits under this Annex;

(f) "permit" means a formal permission in writing issued by an appropriate authority;

(g) "take" or "taking" means to kill, injure, capture, handle or molest a native mammal or bird, or to remove or damage such quantities of native plants or invertebrates that their local distribution or abundance would be significantly affected;

(h) "harmful interference" means:

    (i) flying or landing helicopters or other aircraft in a manner that disturbs concentrations of native birds or seals;

    (ii) using vehicles or vessels, including hovercraft and small boats, in a manner that disturbs concentrations of native birds or seals;

    (iii) using explosives or firearms in a manner that disturbs concentrations of native birds or seals;

    (iv) wilfully disturbing breeding or moulting native birds or concentrations of native birds or seals by persons on foot;

    (v) significantly damaging concentrations of native terrestrial plants by landing aircraft, driving vehicles, or walking on them, or by other means; and

    (vi) any activity that results in the significant adverse modification of habitats of any species or population of native mammal, bird, plant or invertebrate.

(i) "International Convention for the Regulation of Whaling" means the Convention done at Washington on 2 December 1946.

(j) "Agreement on the Conservation of Albatrosses and Petrels" means the Agreement done at Canberra on 19 June 2001.

ARTICLE 2

CASES OF EMERGENCY

1. This Annex shall not apply in cases of emergency relating to the safety of human life or of ships, aircraft, or equipment and facilities of high value, or the protection of the environment.

2. Notice of activities undertaken in cases of emergency that result in any taking or harmful interference shall be circulated immediately to all Parties and to the Committee.

ARTICLE 3

PROTECTION OF NATIVE FAUNA AND FLORA

1. Taking or harmful interference shall be prohibited, except in accordance with a permit.

2. Such permits shall specify the authorised activity, including when, where and by whom it is to be conducted and shall be issued only in the following circumstances:

(a) to provide specimens for scientific study or scientific information;

(b) to provide specimens for museums, herbaria and botanical gardens, or other educational institutions or uses;

(c) to provide specimens for zoological gardens but, in respect of native mammals or birds, only if such specimens cannot be obtained from existing captive collections elsewhere, or if there is a compelling conservation requirement; and

(d)   to provide for unavoidable consequences of scientific activities not otherwise authorised under sub-paragraphs (a), (b) or (c) above, or of the construction and operation of scientific support facilities.

3.   The issue of such permits shall be limited so as to ensure that:

(a)   no more native mammals, birds, plants or invertebrates are taken than are strictly necessary to meet the purposes set forth in paragraph 2 above;

(b)   only small numbers of native mammals or birds are killed, and in no case more are killed from local populations than can, in combination with other permitted takings, normally be replaced by natural reproduction in the following season; and

(c)   the diversity of species, as well as the habitats essential to their existence, and the balance of the ecological systems existing within the Antarctic Treaty area are maintained.

4.   Any species of native mammals, birds, plants and invertebrates listed in Appendix A to this Annex shall be designated "Specially Protected Species", and shall be accorded special protection by the Parties.

5.   Designation of a species as a Specially Protected Species shall be undertaken according to agreed procedures and criteria adopted by the ATCM.

6.   The Committee shall review and provide advice on the criteria for proposing native mammals, birds, plants or invertebrates for designation as a Specially Protected Species.

7.   Any Party, the Committee, the Scientific Committee on Antarctic Research or the Commission for the Conservation of Antarctic Marine Living Resources may propose a species for designation as a Specially Protected Species by submitting a proposal with justification to the ATCM.

8.   A permit shall not be issued to a Specially Protected Species unless the taking:

(a)   is for a compelling scientific purpose; and

(b)   will not jeopardise the survival or recovery of that species or local population;

9.   The use of lethal techniques on Specially Protected Species shall only be permitted where there is no suitable alternative technique.

10.   Proposals for the designation of a species as a Specially Protected Species shall be forwarded to the Committee, the Scientific Committee on Antarctic Research and, for native mammals and birds, the Commission for the Conservation of Antarctic Marine Living Resources, and as appropriate, the Meeting of the Parties to

the Agreement on the Conservation of Albatrosses and Petrels and other organisations. In formulating its advice to the ATCM on whether a species should be designated as a Specially Protected Species, the Committee shall take into account any comments provided by the Scientific Committee on Antarctic Research, and, for native mammals and birds, the Commission for the Conservation of Antarctic Marine Living Resources, and as appropriate, the Meeting of the Parties to the Agreement on the Conservation of Albatrosses and Petrels and other organisations.

11.   All taking of native mammals and birds shall be done in the manner that involves the least degree of pain and suffering practicable.

ARTICLE 4
INTRODUCTION OF NON-NATIVE SPECIES AND DISEASES

1.   No species of living organisms not native to the Antarctic Treaty area shall be introduced onto land or ice shelves, or into water, in the Antarctic Treaty area except in accordance with a permit.

2.   Dogs shall not be introduced onto land, ice shelves or sea ice.

3.   Permits under paragraph 1 above shall:

(a)   be issued to allow the importation only of cultivated plants and their reproductive propagules for controlled use, and species of living organisms for controlled experimental use; and

(b)   specify the species numbers and, if appropriate, age and sex of the species to be introduced, along with a rationale, justifying the introduction and precautions to be taken to prevent escape or contact with fauna or flora.

4.   Any species for which a permit has been issued in accordance with paragraphs 1 and 3 above shall, prior to expiration of the permit, be removed from the Antarctic Treaty area or be disposed of by incineration or equally effective means that eliminates risk to native fauna or flora. The permit shall specify this obligation.

5.   Any species, including progeny, not native to the Antarctic Treaty area that is introduced into that area without a permit that has been issued in accordance with paragraph 1 and 3 above, shall be removed or disposed of whenever feasible, unless the removal or disposal would result in a greater adverse environmental impact. Such removal or disposal may include by incineration or by equally effective means, so as to be rendered sterile, unless it is determined that they pose no risk to native flora or fauna. In addition, all reasonable steps shall be taken to control the consequences of that introduction to avoid harm to native fauna or flora.

6.   Nothing in this Article shall apply to the importation of food into the Antarctic Treaty area provided that no live animals are imported for this purpose and all plants and animal parts and products are kept under carefully controlled conditions and disposed of in accordance with Annex III to the Protocol.

7.   Each Party shall require that precautions are taken to prevent the accidental introduction of micro-organisms (e.g., viruses, bacteria, yeasts, fungi) not present naturally in the Antarctic Treaty area.

8.   No live poultry or other living birds shall be brought into the Antarctic Treaty area. All appropriate efforts shall be made to ensure that poultry or avian products imported into Antarctica are free from contamination by diseases (such as Newcastle's Disease, tuberculosis, and yeast infection) which might be harmful to native flora and fauna. Any poultry or avian products not consumed shall be removed from the Antarctic Treaty area or disposed of by incineration or equivalent means that eliminates the risks of introduction of micro-organisms (e.g. viruses, bacteria, yeasts, fungi) to native flora and fauna.

9.   The deliberate introduction of non-sterile soil into the Antarctic Treaty area is prohibited. Parties should, to the maximum extent practicable, ensure that non-sterile soil is not unintentionally imported into the Antarctic Treaty area.

ARTICLE 5
INFORMATION

Each Party shall make publicly available information on prohibited activities and Specially Protected Species to all those persons present in or intending to enter the Antarctic Treaty area with a view to ensuring that such persons understand and observe the provisions of this Annex.

ARTICLE 6
EXCHANGE OF INFORMATION

1.   The Parties shall make arrangements for:

(a)   collecting and annually exchanging records (including records of permits) and statistics concerning the numbers or quantities of each species of native mammal, bird, plant or invertebrate taken in the Antarctic Treaty area; and

(b)   obtaining and exchanging information as to the status of native mammals, birds, plants, and invertebrates in the Antarctic Treaty area, and the extent to which any species or population needs protection.

2.   As early as possible, after the end of each austral summer season, but in all cases before 1 October of each year, the Parties shall inform the other Parties as well as the Committee of any step taken pursuant to paragraph 1 above and of the number and nature of permits issued under this Annex in the preceding period of 1 April to 31 March.

ARTICLE 7
RELATIONSHIP WITH OTHER AGREEMENTS OUTSIDE THE ANTARCTIC TREATY SYSTEM

Nothing in this Annex shall derogate from the rights and obligations of Parties under the International Convention for the Regulation of Whaling.

ARTICLE 8
REVIEW

The Parties shall keep under continuing review measures for the conservation of Antarctic fauna and flora, taking into account any recommendations from the Committee.

ARTICLE 9
AMENDMENT OR MODIFICATION

1.   This Annex may be amended or modified by a measure adopted in accordance with Article IX (1) of the Antarctic Treaty. Unless the measure specifies otherwise, the amendment or modification shall be deemed to have been approved, and shall become effective, one year after the close of the Antarctic Treaty Consultative Meeting at which it was adopted, unless one or more of the Antarctic Treaty Consultative Parties notifies the Depositary, within that time period, that it wishes an extension of that period or that it is unable to approve the measure.

2.   Any amendment or modification of this Annex which becomes effective in accordance with paragraph 1 above shall thereafter become effective as to any other Party when notice of approval by it has been received by the Depositary.

APPENDICES TO THE ANNEX

APPENDIX A:
SPECIALLY PROTECTED SPECIES

Ommatophoca rossii, Ross Seal.

ANNEX III TO THE PROTOCOL ON ENVIRONMENTAL PROTECTION TO THE ANTARCTIC TREATY

WASTE DISPOSAL AND WASTE MANAGEMENT

ARTICLE 1
GENERAL OBLIGATIONS

1. This Annex shall apply to activities undertaken in the Antarctic Treaty area pursuant to scientific research programmes, tourism and all other governmental and non-governmental activities in the Antarctic Treaty area for which advance notice is required under Article VII (5) of the Antarctic Treaty, including associated logistic support activities.

2. The amount of wastes produced or disposed of in the Antarctic Treaty area shall be reduced as far as practicable so as to minimise impact on the Antarctic environment and to minimise interference with the natural values of Antarctica, with scientific research and with other uses of Antarctica which are consistent with the Antarctic Treaty.

3. Waste storage, disposal and removal from the Antarctic Treaty area, as well as recycling and source reduction, shall be essential considerations in the planning and conduct of activities in the Antarctic Treaty area.

4. Wastes removed from the Antarctic Treaty area shall, to the maximum extent practicable, be returned to the country from which the activities generating the waste were organized or to any other country in which arrangements have been made for the disposal of such wastes in accordance with relevant international agreements.

5. Past and present waste disposal sites on land and abandoned work sites of Antarctic activities shall be cleaned up by the generator of such wastes and the user of such sites. This obligation shall not be interpreted as requiring:

   (a) the removal of any structure designated as a historic site or monument; or

   (b) the removal of any structure or waste material in circumstances where the removal by any practical option would result in greater adverse environmental impact than leaving the structure or waste material in its existing location.

ARTICLE 2

WASTE DISPOSAL BY REMOVAL FROM THE ANTARCTIC TREATY AREA

1.   The following wastes, if generated after entry into force of this Annex, shall be removed from the Antarctic Treaty area by the generator of such wastes:

(a)   radio-active materials;

(b)   electrical batteries;

(c)   fuel, both liquid and solid;

(d)   wastes containing harmful levels of heavy metals or acutely toxic or harmful persistent compounds;

(e)   poly-vinyl chloride (PVC), polyurethane foam, polystyrene foam, rubber and lubricating oils, treated timbers and other products which contain additives that could produce harmful emissions if incinerated;

(f)   all other plastic wastes, except low density polyethylene containers (such as bags for storing wastes), provided that such containers shall be incinerated in accordance with Article 3 (1);

(g)   fuel drums; and

(h)   other solid, non-combustible wastes;

provided that the obligation to remove drums and solid non-combustible wastes contained in subparagraphs (g) and (h) above shall not apply in circumstances where the removal of such wastes by any practical option would result in greater adverse environmental impact than leaving them in their existing locations.

2.   Liquid wastes which are not covered by paragraph 1 above and sewage and domestic liquid wastes, shall, to the maximum extent practicable, be removed from the Antarctic Treaty area by the generator of such wastes.

3.   The following wastes shall be removed from the Antarctic Treaty area by the generator of such wastes, unless incinerated, autoclaved or otherwise treated to be made sterile:

(a)   residues of carcasses of imported animals;

(b)   laboratory culture of micro-organisms and plant pathogens; and

(c)   introduced avian products.

ARTICLE 3

WASTE DISPOSAL BY INCINERATION

1.   Subject to paragraph 2 below, combustible wastes, other than those referred to in Article 2 (1), which are not removed from the Antarctic Treaty area shall be burnt in incinerators which to the maximum extent practicable reduce harmful emissions. Any emission standards and equipment guidelines which may be recommended by, *inter alia*, the Committee and the Scientific Committee on Antarctic Research shall be taken into account. The solid residue of such incineration shall be removed from the Antarctic Treaty area.

2.   All open burning of wastes shall be phased out as soon as practicable, but no later than the end of the 1998/1999 season. Pending the completion of such phase-out, when it is necessary to dispose of wastes by open burning, allowance shall be made for the wind direction and speed and the type of wastes to be burnt to limit particulate deposition and to avoid such deposition over areas of special biological, scientific, historic, aesthetic or wilderness significance including, in particular, areas accorded protection under the Antarctic Treaty.

ARTICLE 4

OTHER WASTE DISPOSAL ON LAND

1.   Wastes not removed or disposed of in accordance with Articles 2 and 3 shall not be disposed of onto ice-free areas or into fresh water systems.

2.   Sewage, domestic liquid wastes and other liquid wastes not removed from the Antarctic Treaty area in accordance with Article 2, shall, to the maximum extent practicable, not be disposed of onto sea ice, ice shelves or the grounded ice-sheet, provided that such wastes which are generated by stations located inland on ice shelves or on the grounded ice-sheet may be disposed of in deep ice pits where such disposal is the only practicable option. Such pits shall not be located on known ice-flow lines which terminate at ice-free areas or in areas of high ablation.

3.   Wastes generated at field camps shall, to the maximum extent practicable, be removed by the generator of such wastes to supporting stations or ships for disposal in accordance with this Annex.

ARTICLE 5

DISPOSAL OF WASTE IN THE SEA

1.   Sewage and domestic liquid wastes may be discharged directly into the sea, taking into account the assimilative capacity of the receiving marine environment and provided that:

(a)   such discharge is located, wherever practicable, where conditions exist for initial dilution and rapid dispersal; and

(b)   large quantities of such wastes (generated in a station where the average weekly occupancy over the austral summer is approximately 30 individuals or more) shall be treated at least by maceration.

2.   The by-product of sewage treatment by the Rotary Biological Contacter process or similar processes may be disposed of into the sea provided that such disposal does not adversely affect the local environment, and provided also that any such disposal at sea shall be in accordance with Annex IV to the Protocol.

ARTICLE 6

STORAGE OF WASTE

All wastes to be removed from the Antarctic Treaty area, or otherwise disposed of, shall be stored in such a way as to prevent their dispersal into the environment.

ARTICLE 7

PROHIBITED PRODUCTS

No polychlorinated biphenyls (PCBs), non-sterile soil, polystyrene beads, chips or similar forms of packaging, or pesticides (other than those required for scientific, medical or hygiene purposes) shall be introduced onto land or ice shelves or into water in the Antarctic Treaty area.

ARTICLE 8

WASTE MANAGEMENT PLANNING

1.   Each Party which itself conducts activities in the Antarctic Treaty area shall, in respect of those activities, establish a waste disposal classification system as a basis for recording wastes and to facilitate studies aimed at evaluating the environmental impacts of scientific activity and associated logistic support. To that end, wastes produced shall be classified as:

(a)   sewage and domestic liquid wastes (Group 1);

(b)   other liquid wastes and chemicals, including fuels and lubricants (Group 2);

(c)   solids to be combusted (Group 3);

(d)   other solid wastes (Group 4); and

(e)   radioactive material (Group 5).

2.   In order to reduce further the impact of waste on the Antarctic environment, each such Party shall prepare and annually review and update its waste management plans (including waste reduction, storage and disposal), specifying for each fixed site, for field camps generally, and for each ship (other than small boats that are part of the operations of fixed sites or of ships and taking into account existing management plans for ships):

(a)   programmes for cleaning up existing waste disposal sites and abandoned work sites;

(b)   current and planned waste management arrangements, including final disposal;

(c)   current and planned arrangements for analysing the environmental effects of waste and waste management; and

(d)   other efforts to minimise any environmental effects of wastes and waste management.

3.   Each such Party shall, as far as is practicable, also prepare an inventory of locations of past activities (such as traverses, field depots, field bases, crashed aircraft) before the information is lost, so that such locations can be taken into account in planning future scientific programmes (such as snow chemistry, pollutants in lichens or ice core drilling).

ARTICLE 9
CIRCULATION AND REVIEW OF WASTE MANAGEMENT PLANS

1.   The waste management plans prepared in accordance with Article 8, reports on their implementation, and the inventories referred to in Article 8 (3), shall be included in the annual exchanges of information in accordance with Articles III and VII of the Antarctic Treaty and related Recommendations under Article IX of the Antarctic Treaty.

2.   Each Party shall send copies of its waste management plans, and reports on their implementation and review, to the Committee.

3.   The Committee may review waste management plans and reports thereon and may offer comments, including suggestions for minimising impacts and modifications and improvement to the plans, for the consideration of the Parties.

4.   The Parties may exchange information and provide advice on, *inter alia*, available low waste technologies, reconversion of existing installations, special requirements for effluents, and appropriate disposal and discharge methods.

ARTICLE 10
MANAGEMENT PRACTICES

Each Party shall:

(a)   designate a waste management official to develop and monitor waste management plans; in the field, this responsibility shall be delegated to an appropriate person at each site;

(b)   ensure that members of its expeditions receive training designed to limit the impact of its operations on the Antarctic environment and to inform them of requirements of this Annex; and

(c)   discourage the use of poly-vinyl chloride (PVC) products and ensure that its expeditions to the Antarctic Treaty are advised of any PVC products they may introduce into that area in order that these products may be removed subsequently in accordance with this Annex.

ARTICLE 11
REVIEW

This Annex shall be subject to regular review in order to ensure that it is updated to reflect improvement in waste disposal technology and procedures and to ensure thereby maximum protection of the Antarctic environment.

ARTICLE 12
CASES OF EMERGENCY

1.   This Annex shall not apply in cases of emergency relating to the safety of human life or of ships, aircraft or equipment and facilities of high value or the protection of the environment.

2.   Notice of activities undertaken in cases of emergency shall be circulated immediately to all Parties and to the Committee.

ARTICLE 13

AMENDMENT OR MODIFICATION

1.   This Annex may be amended or modified by a measure adopted in accordance with Article IX (1) of the Antarctic Treaty. Unless the measure specifies otherwise, the amendment or modification shall be deemed to have been approved, and shall become effective, one year after the close of the Antarctic Treaty Consultative Meeting at which it was adopted, unless one or more of the Antarctic Treaty Consultative Parties notifies the Depositary, within that time period, that it wishes an extension of that period or that it is unable to approve the amendment.

2.   Any amendment or modification of this Annex which becomes effective in accordance with paragraph 1 above shall thereafter become effective as to any other Party when notice of approval by it has been received by the Depositary.

ANNEX IV TO THE PROTOCOL ON ENVIRONMENTAL PROTECTION TO THE ANTARCTIC TREATY

PREVENTION OF MARINE POLLUTION

ARTICLE 1

DEFINITIONS

For the purposes of this Annex:

(a)   "discharge" means any release howsoever caused from a ship and includes any escape, disposal, spilling, leaking, pumping, emitting or emptying;

(b)   "garbage" means all kinds of victual, domestic and operational waste excluding fresh fish and parts thereof, generated during the normal operation of the ship, except those substances which are covered by Articles 3 and 4;

(c)   "MARPOL 73/78" means the International Convention for the Prevention of Pollution from Ships, 1973, as amended by the Protocol of 1978 relating thereto and by any other amendment in force thereafter;

(d)   "noxious liquid substance" means any noxious liquid substance as defined in Annex II of MARPOL 73/78;

(e)   "oil" means petroleum in any form including crude oil, fuel oil, sludge, oil refuse and refined oil products (other than petrochemicals which are subject to the provisions of Article 4);

(f)   "oily mixture" means a mixture with any oil content; and

(g)   "ship" means a vessel of any type whatsoever operating in the marine environment and includes hydrofoil boats, air-cushion vehicles, submersibles, floating craft and fixed or floating platforms.

ARTICLE 2

APPLICATION

This Annex applies, with respect to each Party, to ships entitled to fly its flag and to any other ship engaged in or supporting its Antarctic operations, while operating in the Antarctic Treaty area.

ARTICLE 3
Discharge of Oil

1.   Any discharge into the sea of oil or oily mixture shall be prohibited, except in cases permitted under Annex I of MARPOL 73/78. While operating in the Antarctic Treaty area, ships shall retain on board all sludge, dirty ballast, tank washing waters and other oily residues and mixtures which may not be discharged into the sea. Ships shall discharge these residues only outside the Antarctic Treaty area, at reception facilities or as otherwise permitted under Annex I of MARPOL 73/78.

2.   This Article shall not apply to:

    (a)   the discharge into the sea of oil or oily mixture resulting from damage to a ship or its equipment:

        (i)   provided that all reasonable precautions have been taken after the occurrence of the damage or discovery of the discharge for the purpose of preventing or minimising the discharge; and

        (ii)   except if the owner or the Master acted either with intent to cause damage, or recklessly and with the knowledge that damage would probably result; or

    (b)   the discharge into the sea of substances containing oil which are being used for the purpose of combating specific pollution incidents in order to minimise the damage from pollution.

ARTICLE 4
Discharge of Noxious Liquid Substances

The discharge into the sea of any noxious liquid substance, and any other chemical or other substances, in quantities or concentrations that are harmful to the marine environment, shall be prohibited.

ARTICLE 5
Disposal of Garbage

1.   The disposal into the sea of all plastics, including but not limited to synthetic ropes, synthetic fishing nets, and plastic garbage bags, shall be prohibited.

2.   The disposal into the sea of all other garbage, including paper products, rags, glass, metal, bottles, crockery, incineration ash, dunnage, lining and packing materials, shall be prohibited.

3.   The disposal into the sea of food wastes may be permitted when they have been passed through a comminuter or grinder, provided that such disposal shall, except in cases permitted under Annex V of MARPOL 73/78, be made as far as practicable from land and ice shelves but in any case not less than 12 nautical miles from the nearest land or ice shelf. Such comminuted or ground food wastes shall be capable of passing through a screen with openings no greater than 25 millimeters.

4.   When a substance or material covered by this article is mixed with other such substance or material for discharge or disposal, having different disposal or discharge requirements, the most stringent disposal or discharge requirements shall apply.

5.   The provisions of paragraphs 1 and 2 above shall not apply to:

(a)   the escape of garbage resulting from damage to a ship or its equipment provided all reasonable precautions have been taken, before and after the occurrence of the damage, for the purpose of preventing or minimising the escape; or

(b)   the accidental loss of synthetic fishing nets, provided all reasonable precautions have been taken to prevent such loss.

6.   The Parties shall, where appropriate, require the use of garbage record books.

ARTICLE 6
DISCHARGE OF SEWAGE

1.   Except where it would unduly impair Antarctic operations:

(a)   each Party shall eliminate all discharge into the sea of untreated sewage ("sewage" being defined in Annex IV of MARPOL 73/78) within 12 nautical miles of land or ice shelves;

(b)   beyond such distance, sewage stored in a holding tank shall not be discharged instantaneously but at a moderate rate and, where practicable, while the ship is en route at a speed of no less than 4 knots.

This paragraph does not apply to ships certified to carry not more than 10 persons.

2.   The Parties shall, where appropriate, require the use of sewage record books.

ARTICLE 7
CASES OF EMERGENCY

1.   Articles 3, 4, 5 and 6 of this Annex shall not apply in cases of emergency relating to the safety of a ship and those on board or saving life at sea.

2.   Notice of activities undertaken in cases of emergency shall be circulated immediately to all Parties and to the Committee.

ARTICLE 8
EFFECT ON DEPENDENT AND ASSOCIATED ECOSYSTEMS

In implementing the provisions of this Annex, due consideration shall be given to the need to avoid detrimental effects on dependent and associated ecosystems, outside the Antarctic Treaty area.

ARTICLE 9
SHIP RETENTION CAPACITY AND RECEPTION FACILITIES

1.   Each Party shall undertake to ensure that all ships entitled to fly its flag and any other ship engaged in or supporting its Antarctic operations, before entering the Antarctic Treaty area, are fitted with a tank or tanks of sufficient capacity on board for the retention of all sludge, dirty ballast, tank washing water and other oily residues and mixtures, and have sufficient capacity on board for the retention of garbage, while operating in the Antarctic Treaty area and have concluded arrangements to discharge such oily residues and garbage at a reception facility after leaving that area. Ships shall also have sufficient capacity on board for the retention of noxious liquid substances.

2.   Each Party at whose ports ships depart en route to or arrive from the Antarctic Treaty area undertakes to ensure that as soon as practicable adequate facilities are provided for the reception of all sludge, dirty ballast, tank washing water, other oily residues and mixtures, and garbage from ships, without causing undue delay, and according to the needs of the ships using them.

3.   Parties operating ships which depart to or arrive from the Antarctic Treaty area at ports of other Parties shall consult with those Parties with a view to ensuring that the establishment of port reception facilities does not place an inequitable burden on Parties adjacent to the Antarctic Treaty area.

ARTICLE 10
DESIGN, CONSTRUCTION, MANNING AND EQUIPMENT OF SHIPS

In the design, construction, manning and equipment of ships engaged in or supporting Antarctic operations, each Party shall take into account the objectives of this Annex.

ARTICLE 11
SOVEREIGN IMMUNITY

1.   This Annex shall not apply to any warship, naval auxiliary or other ship owned or operated by a State and used, for the time being, only on government non-commercial service. However, each Party shall ensure by the adoption of appropriate

measures not impairing the operations or operational capabilities of such ships owned or operated by it, that such ships act in a manner consistent, so far as is reasonable and practicable, with this Annex.

2.   In applying paragraph 1 above, each Party shall take into account the importance of protecting the Antarctic environment.

3.   Each Party shall inform the other Parties of how it implements this provision.

4.   The dispute settlement procedure set out in Articles 18 to 20 of the Protocol shall not apply to this Article.

ARTICLE 12
PREVENTIVE MEASURES AND EMERGENCY PREPAREDNESS AND RESPONSE

1.   In order to respond more effectively to marine pollution emergencies or the threat thereof in the Antarctic Treaty area, the Parties, in accordance with Article 15 of the Protocol, shall develop contingency plans for marine pollution response in the Antarctic Treaty area, including contingency plans for ships (other than small boats that are part of the operations of fixed sites or of ships) operating in the Antarctic Treaty area, particularly ships carrying oil as cargo, and for oil spills, originating from coastal installations, which enter into the marine environment. To this end they shall:

(a)   co-operate in the formulation and implementation of such plans; and

(b)   draw on the advice of the Committee, the International Maritime Organization and other international organizations.

2.   The Parties shall also establish procedures for cooperative response to pollution emergencies and shall take appropriate response actions in accordance with such procedures.

ARTICLE 13
REVIEW

The Parties shall keep under continuous review the provisions of this Annex and other measures to prevent, reduce and respond to pollution of the Antarctic marine environment, including any amendments and new regulations adopted under MARPOL 73/78, with a view to achieving the objectives of this Annex.

ARTICLE 14
RELATIONSHIP WITH MARPOL 73/78

With respect to those Parties which are also Parties to MARPOL 73/78, nothing in this Annex shall derogate from the specific rights and obligations thereunder.

ARTICLE 15
AMENDMENT OR MODIFICATION

1.   This Annex may be amended or modified by a measure adopted in accordance with Article IX (1) of the Antarctic Treaty. Unless the measure specifies otherwise, the amendment or modification shall be deemed to have been approved, and shall become effective, one year after the close of the Antarctic Treaty Consultative Meeting at which it was adopted, unless one or more of the Antarctic Treaty Consultative Parties notifies the Depositary, within that time period, that it wishes an extension of that period or that it is unable to approve the measure.

2.   Any amendment or modification of this Annex which becomes effective in accordance with paragraph 1 above shall thereafter become effective as to any other Party when notice of approval by it has been received by the Depositary.

ANNEX TO RECOMMENDATION XVI-10

ANNEX V
TO THE PROTOCOL ON ENVIRONMENTAL PROTECTION
TO THE ANTARCTIC TREATY

AREA PROTECTION AND MANAGEMENT

ARTICLE 1
DEFINITIONS

For the purposes of this Annex:

(a) "appropriate authority" means any person or agency authorised by a Party to issue permits under this Annex;

(b) "permit" means a formal permission in writing issued by an appropriate authority;

(c) "Management Plan" means a plan to manage the activities and protect the special value or values in an Antarctic Specially Protected Area or an Antarctic Specially Managed Area.

ARTICLE 2
OBJECTIVES

For the purposes set out in this Annex, any area, including any marine area, may be designated as an Antarctic Specially Protected Area or an Antarctic Specially Managed Area. Activities in those Areas shall be prohibited, restricted or managed in accordance with Management Plans adopted under the provisions of this Annex.

ARTICLE 3
ANTARCTIC SPECIALLY PROTECTED AREAS

1.   Any area, including any marine area, may be designated as an Antarctic Specially Protected Area to protect outstanding environmental, scientific, historic, aesthetic or wilderness values, any combination of those values, or ongoing or planned scientific research.

2.   Parties shall seek to identify, within a systematic environmental-geographical framework, and to include in the series of Antarctic Specially Protected Areas:

(a) areas kept inviolate from human interference so that future comparisons may be possible with localities that have been affected by human activities;

(b) representative examples of major terrestrial, including glacial and aquatic, ecosystems and marine ecosystems;

(c) areas with important or unusual assemblages of species, including major colonies of breeding native birds or mammals;

(d) the type locality or only known habitat of any species;

(e) areas of particular interest to ongoing or planned scientific research;

(f) examples of outstanding geological, glaciological or geomorphological features;

(g) areas of outstanding aesthetic and wilderness value;

(h) sites or monuments of recognised historic value; and

(i) such other areas as may be appropriate to protect the values set out in paragraph 1 above.

3. Specially Protected Areas and Sites of Special Scientific Interest designated as such by past Antarctic Treaty Consultative Meetings are hereby designated as Antarctic Specially Protected Areas and shall be renamed and renumbered accordingly.

4. Entry into an Antarctic Specially Protected Area shall be prohibited except in accordance with a permit issued under Article 7.

ARTICLE 4
ANTARCTIC SPECIALLY MANAGED AREAS

1. Any area, including any marine area, where activities are being conducted or may in the future be conducted, may be designated as an Antarctic Specially Managed Area to assist in the planning and co-ordination of activities, avoid possible conflicts, improve co-operation between Parties or minimise environmental impacts.

2. Antarctic Specially Managed Areas may include:

(a) areas where activities pose risks of mutual interference or cumulative environmental impacts; and

(b) sites or monuments of recognised historic value.

3. Entry into an Antarctic Specially Managed Area shall not require a permit.

4. Notwithstanding paragraph 3 above, an Antarctic Specially Managed Area may contain one or more Antarctic Specially Protected Areas, entry into which shall be prohibited except in accordance with a permit issued under Article 7.

ARTICLE 5
MANAGEMENT PLANS

1.   Any Party, the Committee, the Scientific Committee for Antarctic Research or the Commission for the Conservation of Antarctic Marine Living Resources may propose an area for designation as an Antarctic Specially Protected Area or an Antarctic Specially Managed Area by submitting a proposed Management Plan to the Antarctic Treaty Consultative Meeting.

2.   The area proposed for designation shall be of sufficient size to protect the values for which the special protection or management is required.

3.   Proposed Management Plans shall include, as appropriate:

(a)   a description of the value or values for which special protection or management is required;

(b)   a statement of the aims and objectives of the Management Plan for the protection or management of those values;

(c)   management activities which are to be undertaken to protect the values for which special protection or management is required;

(d)   a period of designation, if any;

(e)   a description of the area, including:

    (i)   the geographical co-ordinates, boundary markers and natural features that delineate the area;

    (ii)   access to the area by land, sea or air including marine approaches and anchorages, pedestrian and vehicular routes within the area, and aircraft routes and landing areas;

    (iii)   the location of structures, including scientific stations, research or refuge facilities, both within the area and near to it; and

    (iv)   the location in or near the area of other Antarctic Specially Protected Areas or Antarctic Specially Managed Areas designated under this Annex, or other protected areas designated in accordance with measures adopted under other components of the Antarctic Treaty system;

(f)   the identification of zones within the area, in which activities are to be prohibited, restricted or managed for the purpose of achieving the aims and objectives referred to in subparagraph (b) above;

(g)   maps and photographs that show clearly the boundary of the area in relation to surrounding features and key features within the area;

(h)   supporting documentation;

(i) in respect of an area proposed for designation as an Antarctic Specially Protected Area, a clear description of the conditions under which permits may be granted by the appropriate authority regarding:

(i) access to and movement within or over the area;

(ii) activities which are or may be conducted within the area, including restrictions on time and place;

(iii) the installation, modification, or removal of structures;

(iv) the location of field camps;

(v) restrictions on materials and organisms which may be brought into the area;

(vi) the taking of or harmful interference with native flora and fauna;

(vii) the collection or removal of anything not brought into the area by the permit-holder;

(viii) the disposal of waste;

(ix) measures that may be necessary to ensure that the aims and objectives of the Management Plan can continue to be met; and

(x) requirements for reports to be made to the appropriate authority regarding visits to the area;

(j) in respect of an area proposed for designation as an Antarctic Specially Managed Area, a code of conduct regarding:

(i) access to and movement within or over the area;

(ii) activities which are or may be conducted within the area, including restrictions on time and place;

(iii) the installation, modification, or removal of structures;

(iv) the location of field camps;

(v) the taking of or harmful interference with native flora and fauna;

(vi) the collection or removal of anything not brought into the area by the visitor;

(vii) the disposal of waste; and

(viii) any requirements for reports to be made to the appropriate authority regarding visits to the area; and

(k) provisions relating to the circumstances in which Parties should seek to exchange information in advance of activities which they propose to conduct.

ARTICLE 6

DESIGNATION PROCEDURES

1.   Proposed Management Plans shall be forwarded to the Committee, the Scientific Committee on Antarctic Research and, as appropriate, to the Commission for the Conservation of Antarctic Marine Living Resources. In formulating its advice to the Antarctic Treaty Consultative Meeting, the Committee shall take into account any comments provided by the Scientific Committee on Antarctic Research and, as appropriate, by the Commission for the Conservation of Antarctic Marine Living Resources. Thereafter Management Plans may be approved by the Antarctic Treaty Consultative Parties by a measure adopted at an Antarctic Treaty Consultative Meeting in accordance with Article IX (1) of the Antarctic Treaty. Unless the measure specifies otherwise, the Plan shall be deemed to have been approved 90 days after the close of the Antarctic Treaty Consultative Meeting at which it was adopted, unless one or more of the Consultative Parties notifies the Depositary, within that time period, that it wishes an extension of that period or is unable to approve the measure.

2.   Having regard to the provisions of Articles 4 and 5 of the Protocol, no marine area shall be designated as an Antarctic Specially Protected Area or an Antarctic Specially Managed Area without the prior approval of the Commission for the Conservation of Antarctic Marine Living Resources.

3.   Designation of an Antarctic Specially Protected Area or an Antarctic Specially Managed Area shall be for an indefinite period unless the Management Plan provides otherwise. A review of a Management Plan shall be initiated at least every five years. The Plan shall be updated as necessary.

4.   Management Plans may be amended or revoked in accordance with paragraph 1 above.

5.   Upon approval Management Plans shall be circulated promptly by the Depositary to all Parties. The Depositary shall maintain a record of all currently approved Management Plans.

ARTICLE 7

PERMITS

1.   Each Party shall appoint an appropriate authority to issue permits to enter and engage in activities within an Antarctic Specially Protected Area in accordance with the requirements of the Management Plan relating to that Area. The permit shall be accompanied by the relevant sections of the Management Plan and shall specify the extent and location of the Area, the authorised activities and when, where and by whom the activities are authorised and any other conditions imposed by the Management Plan.

2.   In the case of a Specially Protected Area designated as such by past Antarctic Treaty Consultative Meetings which does not have a Management Plan, the appropriate authority may issue a permit for a compelling scientific purpose which cannot be served elsewhere and which will not jeopardise the natural ecological system in that Area.

3.   Each Party shall require a permit-holder to carry a copy of the permit while in the Antarctic Specially Protected Area concerned.

ARTICLE 8

HISTORIC SITES AND MONUMENTS

1.   Sites or monuments of recognised historic value which have been designated as Antarctic Specially Protected Areas or Antarctic Specially Managed Areas, or which are located within such Areas, shall be listed as Historic Sites and Monuments.

2.   Any Party may propose a site or monument of recognised historic value which has not been designated as an Antarctic Specially Protected Area or an Antarctic Specially Managed Area, or which is not located within such an Area, for listing as a Historic Site or Monument. The proposal for listing may be approved by the Antarctic Treaty Consultative Parties by a measure adopted at an Antarctic Treaty Consultative Meeting in accordance with Article IX (1) of the Antarctic Treaty. Unless the measure specifies otherwise, the proposal shall be deemed to have been approved 90 days after the close of the Antarctic Treaty Consultative Meeting at which it was adopted, unless one or more of the Consultative Parties notifies the Depositary, within that time period, that it wishes an extension of that period or is unable to approve the measure.

3.   Existing Historic Sites and Monuments which have been listed as such by previous Antarctic Treaty Consultative Meetings shall be included in the list of Historic Sites and Monuments under this Article.

4.   Listed Historic Sites and Monuments shall not be damaged, removed or destroyed.

5.   The list of Historic Sites and Monuments may be amended in accordance with paragraph 2 above. The Depositary shall maintain a list of current Historic Sites and Monuments.

ARTICLE 9

INFORMATION AND PUBLICITY

1.   With a view to ensuring that all persons visiting or proposing to visit Antarctica understand and observe the provisions of this Annex, each Party shall make available information setting forth, in particular:

(a)   the location of Antarctic Specially Protected Areas and Antarctic Specially Managed Areas;

(b)   listing and maps of those Areas;

(c)   the Management Plans, including listings of prohibitions relevant to each Area;

(d)   the location of Historic Sites and Monuments and any relevant prohibition or restriction.

2.   Each Party shall ensure that the location and, if possible, the limits, of Antarctic Specially Protected Areas, Antarctic Specially Managed Areas and Historic Sites and Monuments are shown on its topographic maps, hydrographic charts and in other relevant publications.

3.   Parties shall co-operate to ensure that, where appropriate, the boundaries of Antarctic Specially Protected Areas, Antarctic Specially Managed Areas and Historic Sites and Monuments are suitably marked on the site.

ARTICLE 10
EXCHANGE OF INFORMATION

1.   The Parties shall make arrangements for:

(a)   collecting and exchanging records, including records of permits and reports of visits, including inspection visits, to Antarctic Specially Protected Areas and reports of inspection visits to Antarctic Specially Managed Areas;

(b)   obtaining and exchanging information on any significant change or damage to any Antarctic Specially Managed Area, Antarctic Specially Protected Area or Historic Site or Monument; and

(c)   establishing common forms in which records and information shall be submitted by Parties in accordance with paragraph 2 below.

2.   Each Party shall inform the other Parties and the Committee before the end of November of each year of the number and nature of permits issued under this Annex in the preceding period of 1st July to 30th June.

3.   Each Party conducting, funding or authorising research or other activities in Antarctic Specially Protected Areas or Antarctic Specially Managed Areas shall maintain a record of such activities and in the annual exchange of information in accordance with the Antarctic Treaty shall provide summary descriptions of the activities conducted by persons subject to its jurisdiction in such areas in the preceding year.

4.   Each Party shall inform the other Parties and the Committee before the end of November each year of measures it has taken to implement this Annex, including any site inspections and any steps it has taken to address instances of activities in

contravention of the provisions of the approved Management Plan for an Antarctic Specially Protected Area or Antarctic Specially Managed Area.

ARTICLE 11
CASES OF EMERGENCY

1.   The restrictions laid down and authorised by this Annex shall not apply in cases of emergency involving safety of human life or of ships, aircraft, or equipment and facilities of high value or the protection of the environment.

2.   Notice of activities undertaken in cases of emergency shall be circulated immediately to all Parties and to the Committee.

ARTICLE 12
AMENDMENT OR MODIFICATION

1.   This Annex may be amended or modified by a measure adopted in accordance with Article IX (1) of the Antarctic Treaty. Unless the measure specifies otherwise, the amendment or modification shall be deemed to have been approved, and shall become effective, one year after the close of the Antarctic Treaty Consultative Meeting at which it was adopted, unless one or more of the Antarctic Treaty Consultative Parties notifies the Depositary, within that time period, that it wishes an extension of that period or that it is unable to approve the measure.

2.   Any amendment or modification of this Annex which becomes effective in accordance with paragraph 1 above shall thereafter become effective as to any other Party when notice of approval by it has been received by the Depositary.

ANNEX VI TO THE PROTOCOL ON ENVIRONMENTAL PROTECTION TO THE ANTARCTIC TREATY

LIABILITY ARISING FROM ENVIRONMENTAL EMERGENCIES

PREAMBLE

The Parties,

Recognising the importance of preventing, minimising and containing the impact of environmental emergencies on the Antarctic environment and dependent and associated ecosystems;

Recalling Article 3 of the Protocol, in particular that activities shall be planned and conducted in the Antarctic Treaty area so as to accord priority to scientific research and to preserve the value of Antarctica as an area for the conduct of such research;

Recalling the obligation in Article 15 of the Protocol to provide for prompt and effective response action to environmental emergencies, and to establish contingency plans for response to incidents with potential adverse effects on the Antarctic environment or dependent and associated ecosystems;

Recalling Article 16 of the Protocol under which the Parties to the Protocol undertook consistent with the objectives of the Protocol for the comprehensive protection of the Antarctic environment and dependent and associated ecosystems to elaborate, in one or more Annexes to the Protocol, rules and procedures relating to liability for damage arising from activities taking place in the Antarctic Treaty area and covered by the Protocol;

Noting further Decision 3 (2001) of the XXIVth Antarctic Treaty Consultative Meeting regarding the elaboration of an Annex on the liability aspects of environmental emergencies, as a step in the establishment of a liability regime in accordance with Article 16 of the Protocol;

Having regard to Article IV of the Antarctic Treaty and Article 8 of the Protocol;

Have agreed as follows:

ARTICLE 1
SCOPE

This Annex shall apply to environmental emergencies in the Antarctic Treaty area which relate to scientific research programmes, tourism and all other governmental and non-governmental activities in the Antarctic Treaty area for which advance notice is required under Article VII(5) of the Antarctic Treaty, including associated logistic support activities. Measures and plans for preventing and responding to such emergencies are also included in this Annex. It shall apply to all tourist vessels that enter the Antarctic Treaty area. It shall also apply to environmental emergencies in the Antarctic Treaty area which relate to other vessels and activities as may be decided in accordance with Article 13.

ARTICLE 2
DEFINITIONS

For the purposes of this Annex:

(a) "Decision" means a Decision adopted pursuant to the Rules of Procedure of Antarctic Treaty Consultative Meetings and referred to in Decision 1 (1995) of the XIXth Antarctic Treaty Consultative Meeting;

(b) "Environmental emergency" means any accidental event that has occurred, having taken place after the entry into force of this Annex, and that results in, or imminently threatens to result in, any significant and harmful impact on the Antarctic environment;

(c) "Operator" means any natural or juridical person, whether governmental or non-governmental, which organises activities to be carried out in the Antarctic Treaty area. An operator does not include a natural person who is an employee, contractor, subcontractor, or agent of, or who is in the service of, a natural or juridical person, whether governmental or non-governmental, which organises activities to be carried out in the Antarctic Treaty area, and does not include a juridical person that is a contractor or subcontractor acting on behalf of a State operator;

(d) "Operator of the Party" means an operator that organises, in that Party's territory, activities to be carried out in the Antarctic Treaty area, and:

(i) those activities are subject to authorisation by that Party for the Antarctic Treaty area; or

(ii) in the case of a Party which does not formally authorise activities for the Antarctic Treaty area, those activities are subject to a comparable regulatory process by that Party.

The terms "its operator", "Party of the operator", and "Party of that operator" shall be interpreted in accordance with this definition;

(e) "Reasonable", as applied to preventative measures and response action, means measures or actions which are appropriate, practicable, proportionate and based on the availability of objective criteria and information, including:

(i) risks to the Antarctic environment, and the rate of its natural recovery;

(ii) risks to human life and safety; and

(iii) technological and economic feasibility;

(f) "Response action" means reasonable measures taken after an environmental emergency has occurred to avoid, minimise or contain the impact of that environmental emergency, which to that end may include clean-up in appropriate circumstances, and includes determining the extent of that emergency and its impact;

(g) "The Parties" means the States for which this Annex has become effective in accordance with Article 9 of the Protocol.

ARTICLE 3
PREVENTATIVE MEASURES

1. Each Party shall require its operators to undertake reasonable preventative measures that are designed to reduce the risk of environmental emergencies and their potential adverse impact.

2. Preventative measures may include:

(a) specialised structures or equipment incorporated into the design and construction of facilities and means of transportation;

(b) specialised procedures incorporated into the operation or maintenance of facilities and means of transportation; and

(c) specialised training of personnel.

ARTICLE 4
CONTINGENCY PLANS

1. Each Party shall require its operators to:

(a)   establish contingency plans for responses to incidents with potential adverse impacts on the Antarctic environment or dependent and associated ecosystems; and

(b)   co-operate in the formulation and implementation of such contingency plans.

2.   Contingency plans shall include, when appropriate, the following components:

(a)   procedures for conducting an assessment of the nature of the incident;

(b)   notification procedures;

(c)   identification and mobilisation of resources;

(d)   response plans;

(e)   training;

(f)   record keeping; and

(g)   demobilisation.

3.   Each Party shall establish and implement procedures for immediate notification of, and co-operative responses to, environmental emergencies, and shall promote the use of notification procedures and co-operative response procedures by its operators that cause environmental emergencies.

ARTICLE 5
RESPONSE ACTION

1.   Each Party shall require each of its operators to take prompt and effective response action to environmental emergencies arising from the activities of that operator.

2.   In the event that an operator does not take prompt and effective response action, the Party of that operator and other Parties are encouraged to take such action, including through their agents and operators specifically authorised by them to take such action on their behalf.

3.   (a) Other Parties wishing to take response action to an environmental emergency pursuant to paragraph 2 above shall notify their intention to the Party of the operator and the Secretariat of the Antarctic Treaty beforehand with a view to the Party of the operator taking response action itself, except where a threat of significant and harmful impact to the Antarctic environment is imminent and it would be reasonable in all the circumstances to take immediate response action, in which case they shall

notify the Party of the operator and the Secretariat of the Antarctic Treaty as soon as possible.

(b) Such other Parties shall not take response action to an environmental emergency pursuant to paragraph 2 above, unless a threat of significant and harmful impact to the Antarctic environment is imminent and it would be reasonable in all the circumstances to take immediate response action, or the Party of the operator has failed within a reasonable time to notify the Secretariat of the Antarctic Treaty that it will take the response action itself, or where that response action has not been taken within a reasonable time after such notification.

(c) In the case that the Party of the operator takes response action itself, but is willing to be assisted by another Party or Parties, the Party of the operator shall coordinate the response action.

4. However, where it is unclear which, if any, Party is the Party of the operator or it appears that there may be more than one such Party, any Party taking response action shall make best endeavours to consult as appropriate and shall, where practicable, notify the Secretariat of the Antarctic Treaty of the circumstances.

5. Parties taking response action shall consult and coordinate their action with all other Parties taking response action, carrying out activities in the vicinity of the environmental emergency, or otherwise impacted by the environmental emergency, and shall, where practicable, take into account all relevant expert guidance which has been provided by permanent observer delegations to the Antarctic Treaty Consultative Meeting, by other organisations, or by other relevant experts.

ARTICLE 6

LIABILITY

1. An operator that fails to take prompt and effective response action to environmental emergencies arising from its activities shall be liable to pay the costs of response action taken by Parties pursuant to Article 5(2) to such Parties.

2. (a) When a State operator should have taken prompt and effective response action but did not, and no response action was taken by any Party, the State operator shall be liable to pay the costs of the response action which should have been undertaken, into the fund referred to in Article 12.

(b) When a non-State operator should have taken prompt and effective response action but did not, and no response action was taken by any Party, the non-State operator shall be liable to pay an amount of money that reflects as much as possible the costs of the response action that should have been taken. Such money is to be paid directly to the fund referred to in Article 12, to the Party of that operator or to the Party that enforces the mechanism referred to in Article 7(3). A Party receiving such money shall make best efforts to make a contribution to the fund referred to in Article 12 which at least equals the money received from the operator.

3. Liability shall be strict.

4. When an environmental emergency arises from the activities of two or more operators, they shall be jointly and severally liable, except that an operator which establishes that only part of the environmental emergency results from its activities shall be liable in respect of that part only.

5. Notwithstanding that a Party is liable under this Article for its failure to provide for prompt and effective response action to environmental emergencies caused by its warships, naval auxiliaries, or other ships or aircraft owned or operated by it and used, for the time being, only on government non-commercial service, nothing in this Annex is intended to affect the sovereign immunity under international law of such warships, naval auxiliaries, or other ships or aircraft.

ARTICLE 7
ACTIONS

1. Only a Party that has taken response action pursuant to Article 5(2) may bring an action against a non-State operator for liability pursuant to Article 6(1) and such action may be brought in the courts of not more than one Party where the operator is incorporated or has its principal place of business or his or her habitual place of residence. However, should the operator not be incorporated in a Party or have its principal place of business or his or her habitual place of residence in a Party, the action may be brought in the courts of the Party of the operator within the meaning of Article 2(d). Such actions for compensation shall be brought within three years of the commencement of the response action or within three years of the date on which the Party bringing the action knew or ought reasonably to have known the identity of the operator, whichever is later. In no event shall an action against a non-State operator be commenced later than 15 years after the commencement of the response action.

2. Each Party shall ensure that its courts possess the necessary jurisdiction to entertain actions under paragraph 1 above.

3. Each Party shall ensure that there is a mechanism in place under its domestic law for the enforcement of Article 6(2)(b) with respect to any of its non-State operators within the meaning of Article 2(d), as well as where possible with respect to any non- State operator that is incorporated or has its principal place of business or his or her habitual place of residence in that Party. Each Party shall inform all other Parties of this mechanism in accordance with Article 13(3) of the Protocol.

Where there are multiple Parties that are capable of enforcing Article 6(2)(b) against any given non- State operator under this paragraph, such Parties should consult amongst themselves as to which Party should take enforcement action. The mechanism referred to in this paragraph shall not be invoked later than 15 years after the date the Party seeking to invoke the mechanism became aware of the environmental emergency.

4.   The liability of a Party as a State operator under Article 6(1) shall be resolved only in accordance with any enquiry procedure which may be established by the Parties, the provisions of Articles 18, 19 and 20 of the Protocol and, as applicable, the Schedule to the Protocol on Arbitration.

5.   (a) The liability of a Party as a State operator under Article 6(2)(a) shall be resolved only by the Antarctic Treaty Consultative Meeting and, should the question remain unresolved, only in accordance with any enquiry procedure which may be established by the Parties, the provisions of Articles 18, 19 and 20 of the Protocol and, as applicable, the Schedule to the Protocol on Arbitration.

       (b) The costs of the response action which should have been undertaken and was not, to be paid by a State operator into the fund referred to in Article 12, shall be approved by means of a Decision. The Antarctic Treaty Consultative Meeting should seek the advice of the Committee on Environmental Protection as appropriate.

6.   Under this Annex, the provisions of Articles 19(4), 19(5), and 20(1) of the Protocol, and, as applicable, the Schedule to the Protocol on Arbitration, are only applicable to liability of a Party as a State operator for compensation for response action that has been undertaken to an environmental emergency or for payment into the fund.

ARTICLE 8

EXEMPTIONS FROM LIABILITY

1.   An operator shall not be liable pursuant to Article 6 if it proves that the environmental emergency was caused by:

       (a) an act or omission necessary to protect human life or safety;

       (b) an event constituting in the circumstances of Antarctica a natural disaster of an exceptional character, which could not have been reasonably foreseen, either generally or in the particular case, provided all reasonable preventative measures have been taken that are designed to reduce the risk of environmental emergencies and their potential adverse impact;

       (c) an act of terrorism; or

       (d) an act of belligerency against the activities of the operator.

2.   A Party, or its agents or operators specifically authorised by it to take such action on its behalf, shall not be liable for an environmental emergency resulting from response action taken by it pursuant to Article 5(2) to the extent that such response action was reasonable in all the circumstances.

ARTICLE 9
LIMITS OF LIABILITY

1.   The maximum amount for which each operator may be liable under Article 6(1) or Article 6(2), in respect of each environmental emergency, shall be as follows:

    (a)   for an environmental emergency arising from an event involving a ship:

        (i)   one million SDR for a ship with a tonnage not exceeding 2,000 tons;

        (ii)   for a ship with a tonnage in excess thereof, the following amount in addition to that referred to in (i) above:

        -    for each ton from 2,001 to 30,000 tons, 400 SDR;
        -    for each ton from 30,001 to 70,000 tons, 300 SDR; and
        -    for each ton in excess of 70,000 tons, 200 SDR;

    (b)   for an environmental emergency arising from an event which does not involve a ship, three million SDR.

2.   (a)   Notwithstanding paragraph 1(a) above, this Annex shall not affect:

        (i)   the liability or right to limit liability under any applicable international limitation of liability treaty; or

        (ii)   the application of a reservation made under any such treaty to exclude the application of the limits therein for certain claims;

    provided that the applicable limits are at least as high as the following: for a ship with a tonnage not exceeding 2,000 tons, one million SDR; and for a ship with a tonnage in excess thereof, in addition, for a ship with a tonnage between 2,001 and 30,000 tons, 400 SDR for each ton; for a ship with a tonnage from 30,001 to 70,000 tons, 300 SDR for each ton; and for each ton in excess of 70,000 tons, 200 SDR for each ton.

    (b)   Nothing in subparagraph (a) above shall affect either the limits of liability set out in paragraph 1(a) above that apply to a Party as a State operator, or the rights and obligations of Parties that are not parties to any such treaty as mentioned above, or the application of Article 7(1) and Article 7(2).

3.   Liability shall not be limited if it is proved that the environmental emergency resulted from an act or omission of the operator, committed with the intent to cause such emergency, or recklessly and with knowledge that such emergency would probably result.

4.   The Antarctic Treaty Consultative Meeting shall review the limits in paragraphs 1(a) and 1(b) above every three years, or sooner at the request of any Party. Any amendments to these limits, which shall be determined after consultation amongst the Parties and on the basis of advice including scientific and technical advice, shall be made under the procedure set out in Article 13(2).

5.   For the purpose of this Article:

(a)   "ship" means a vessel of any type whatsoever operating in the marine environment and includes hydrofoil boats, air-cushion vehicles, submersibles, floating craft and fixed or floating platforms;

(b)   "SDR" means the Special Drawing Rights as defined by the International Monetary Fund;

(c)   a ship's tonnage shall be the gross tonnage calculated in accordance with the tonnage measurement rules contained in Annex I of the International Convention on Tonnage Measurement of Ships, 1969.

ARTICLE 10
STATE LIABILITY

A Party shall not be liable for the failure of an operator, other than its State operators, to take response action to the extent that that Party took appropriate measures within its competence, including the adoption of laws and regulations, administrative actions and enforcement measures, to ensure compliance with this Annex.

ARTICLE 11
INSURANCE AND OTHER FINANCIAL SECURITY

1.   Each Party shall require its operators to maintain adequate insurance or other financial security, such as the guarantee of a bank or similar financial institution, to cover liability under Article 6(1) up to the applicable limits set out in Article 9(1) and Article 9(2).

2.   Each Party may require its operators to maintain adequate insurance or other financial security, such as the guarantee of a bank or similar financial institution, to cover liability under Article 6(2) up to the applicable limits set out in Article 9(1) and Article 9(2).

3.   Notwithstanding paragraphs 1 and 2 above, a Party may maintain self-insurance in respect of its State operators, including those carrying out activities in the furtherance of scientific research.

ARTICLE 12
THE FUND

1.   The Secretariat of the Antarctic Treaty shall maintain and administer a fund, in accordance with Decisions including terms of reference to be adopted by the Parties, to provide, *inter alia*, for the reimbursement of the reasonable and justified costs incurred by a Party or Parties in taking response action pursuant to Article 5(2).

2.   Any Party or Parties may make a proposal to the Antarctic Treaty Consultative Meeting for reimbursement to be paid from the fund. Such a proposal may be approved by the Antarctic Treaty Consultative Meeting, in which case it shall be approved by way of a Decision. The Antarctic Treaty Consultative Meeting may seek the advice of the Committee of Environmental Protection on such a proposal, as appropriate.

3.   Special circumstances and criteria, such as: the fact that the responsible operator was an operator of the Party seeking reimbursement; the identity of the responsible operator remaining unknown or not subject to the provisions of this Annex; the unforeseen failure of the relevant insurance company or financial institution; or an exemption in Article 8 applying, shall be duly taken into account by the Antarctic Treaty Consultative Meeting under paragraph 2 above.

4.   Any State or person may make voluntary contributions to the fund.

ARTICLE 13
AMENDMENT OR MODIFICATION

1.   This Annex may be amended or modified by a Measure adopted in accordance with Article IX (1) of the Antarctic Treaty.

2.   In the case of a Measure pursuant to Article 9(4), and in any other case unless the Measure in question specifies otherwise, the amendment or modification shall be deemed to have been approved, and shall become effective, one year after the close of the Antarctic Treaty Consultative Meeting at which it was adopted, unless one or more Antarctic Treaty Consultative Parties notifies the Depositary, within that time period, that it wishes any extension of that period or that it is unable to approve the Measure.

3.   Any amendment or modification of this Annex which becomes effective in accordance with paragraph 1 or 2 above shall thereafter become effective as to any other Party when notice of approval by it has been received by the Depositary.

CONVENTION ON THE CONSERVATION OF ANTARCTIC MARINE LIVING RESOURCES (CCAMLR)

CONFERENCE ON THE CONSERVATION OF

ANTARCTIC MARINE LIVING RESOURCES

CANBERRA, 7 - 20 MAY 1980

FINAL ACT

I

The Governments of Argentina, Australia, Belgium, Chile, The French Republic, German Democratic Republic, Germany, Federal Republic of, Japan, New Zealand, Norway, Poland, The Republic of South Africa, The Union of Soviet Socialist Republics, The United Kingdom of Great Britain and Northern Ireland, and The United States of America;

having accepted the invitation extended to them by the Government of Australia to participate in a Conference on the Conservation of Antarctic Marine Living Resources, appointed their representatives, advisers and observers who are listed below:

ARGENTINA

Representatives

His Excellency, Ambassador Angel Maria OLIVERI LOPEZ
Director-General of Antarctica and Malvinas,
Ministry of Foreign Affairs,
Buenos Aires

Alternate Representative

His Excellency, Minister Ricardo Pedro QUADRI
Ministry of Foreign Affairs,
Buenos Aires

Delegates

First Secretary, Joaquin Daniel OTERO
Ministry of Foreign Affairs,
Buenos Aires

Third Secretary, Bernardo FERNANDEZ DA SILVA
Ministry of Foreign Affairs,
Buenos Aires

Advisers

Air General (R) Cesar Miguel COMES
National Director of Antarctic,
Ministry of Defence,
Buenos Aires

Rear Admiral (R) Alberto Oscar CASELLAS
Secretary of Marine Affairs,
Buenos Aires

Rear Admiral (R) Cesar A. CASTAGNA
Navy General Headquarters,
Buenos Aires

Lieutenant Colonel Julio V. FUSCALDO
Antarctic Department,
Army General Headquarters,
Buenos Aires

Vice-Commodore (R) Oscar CAMPOS
National Directorate of Antarctic,
Ministry of Defence,
Buenos Aires

Dr Eduardo Robustiano MARENCO
Ministry of Defence,
Buenos Aires

Secretary

Miss Celia Margarita CHACON
Ministry of Foreign Affairs
Buenos Aires

AUSTRALIA

Representative

Mr J.E. RYAN, OBE
Deputy Secretary,
Department of Foreign Affairs

and subsequently

His Excellency Mr K.G. BRENNAN, AO
Australian Ambassador to Switzerland

Alternate Representatives

Mr G.A. BRENNAN
Assistant Legal Adviser,
Department of Foreign Affairs

Mr M.J. McKEOWN,
International Legal Branch,
Department of Foreign Affairs

Mr J. CARLSON
Oil and Gas Division,
Department of National Development and Energy

Mr C.G McCUE
Acting Director
Antarctic Division,
Department of Science and the Environment

Mr H. JITTS
Marine Science Branch,
Department of Science and the Environment

Mr H. BURMESTER
Principal Legal Officer,
Attorney-General's Department

Dr K.R. KERRY
Antarctic Division,
Department of Science and the Environment

Mr B.J. WALKER
Policy Division
Department of Science and the Environment

Mr M. STURMAN
Policy Branch
Fisheries Division
Department of Primary Industry

Mr A. CATON
Acting Director
Resource Management Section
Department of Primary Industry

Mr J. BAILEY
Economic Division
Department of Foreign Affairs

Dr G. BAINES
Australian National Parks & Wildlife Service

Mr G. KAZS
Education and Science Branch
Department of Finance

Mr N. BRIDGER
Government and Legal Branch
Department of the Prime Minister and Cabinet

Mr D.C. McEWAN
Policy Division
Department of Science and the Environment

Mr D.J. MASON
Legal and Treaties Division
Department of Foreign Affairs

Parliamentary Advisers

Senator J. KNIGHT
Senator K.W. SIBRAA
Mr M. BAILLIEU, MP
Mr R. JACOBI, MP

Advisers

Mr A.J. HARRISON
Chairman of the Commonwealth/States Standing Committee on Fisheries

Mr M. KENNEDY
Representative of the Australian Conservation
  Foundation and Friends of the Earth

BELGIUM

Representative

Professor A. van der ESSEN
Minister,
Ministry of Foreign Affairs

Alternate Representative

Mr M.J. COUVREUR
First Secretary,
Belgian Embassy,
Canberra

CHILE

Representative

His Excellency Sr Nicolas NOVOA
Ambassador on Special Mission,
Santiago

Alternate Representatives

His Excellency Sr Jorge VALDOVINOS
Ambassador,
Embassy of the Republic of Chile,
Canberra

Delegates

Sr Juan FONTECILLA
Head of the Antarctic Department,
Directorate of State Boundaries and Limits,
Ministry of Foreign Relations,
Santiago

Sr Carlos CROHARE
Head of Antarctic Division,
Directorate of Special Politics,
Ministry of Foreign Relations,
Santiago

Sr Celso MORENO
Counsellor,
Embassy of the Republic of Chile,
Canberra

Advisers

Sr Roberto CABEZAS
Director, Institute of Fisheries Development,
Economic Ministry,
Santiago

FRANCE

Representative

Mr Rémy TEISSIER du CROS
Ministry Plenipotentiary

Delegation

Mr Daniel HERY
Deputy Director,
Maritime Fisheries,
Ministry of Transport

Miss Josianne COURATIER
Secretary of Foreign Affairs,
Legal Affairs Division,
Ministry of Foreign Affairs

Mr Gerard BOIVINEAU
Second Secretary,
Embassy of France,
Canberra

Adviser

Mr Jean Paul BLOCH
Director of Research,
Secretariat of State of Overseas
Departments and Territories

GERMAN DEMOCRATIC REPUBLIC

Representative

His Excellency Dr Gerhard LINDNER
Ambassador Extraordinary and Plenipotentiary of
German Democratic Republic to Australia

Alternate Representatives

Dr R. POSER
First Secretary,
Embassy of the German Democratic Republic
Canberra

Dr W. RANKE
Ministry of Regionally Administrated and Foodstuff Industries

GERMANY, FEDERAL REPUBLIC OF

Representative

Dr Heinz W. DITTMANN
Ambassador Extraordinary and Plenipotentiary of the
Federal Republic of Germany to Chile

Alternate Representatives

Mr Norbert KLEESCHULTE
Counsellor,
Federal Ministry of Agriculture and Forestry,
Bonn

Dr ARNOLD
Counsellor,
Federal Ministry for Research and Technology,
Bonn

Mr Ingo RADCKE
First Secretary,
Embassy of the Federal Republic of Germany,
Canberra

Mrs Hubertine STEINHAUSEN
Assistant Attache,
Embassy of the Federal Republic of Germany,
Canberra

JAPAN

Representative

His Excellency Mr Mizuo KURODA
Ambassador Extraordinary and Plenipotentiary of Japan
to Australia

Alternate Representatives

Mr Chusei YAMADA
Deputy Director-General,
Treaties Bureau,
Ministry of Foreign Affairs

Mr Takashi TAJIMA
Counsellor (Political)
Embassy of Japan

Mr Fiji KUSANO
Counsellor (Agriculture, Forestry and Fisheries)
Embassy of Japan

Advisers

Mr Tokuya KIKUCHI
Assistant Director,
International Affairs Division,
Oceanic Fishery Department,
Fishery Agency

Mr Keitaro SATO
First Secretary,
Embassy of Japan

Mr Jun YOKOTA
Deputy Director,
International Conventions Division,
Treaties Bureau,
Ministry of Foreign Affairs

Mr Kunio SHIMIZU
Deputy Director,
Fishery Division,
Economic Affairs Bureau,
Ministry of Foreign Affairs

Mr Seigi HINATA
First Secretary
Embassy of Japan

NEW ZEALAND

Representative

Mr W.R. MANSFIELD,
Head, Legal Division,
Ministry of Foreign Affairs,
Wellington

Alternate Representative

Mr A.E. MATHESON
First Secretary,
New Zealand High Commission

NORWAY

Representative

His Excellency Mr Torleiv ANDA
Ambassador

Alternate Representative

Mr H.O. OESTGAARD
Head of Division,
Department of Polar Affairs,
Ministry of Justice and Police

POLAND

Representative

His Excellency Mr Ryszard FRACKIEWICZ
Ambassador Extraordinary and Plenipotentiary of the
Polish People's Republic in Australia

Alternate Representative

Mr Janusz MICKIEWICZ
Director of the Legal and Treaties Department,
Ministry for Foreign Affairs,
Warsaw

Delegates

Mr Jan PIECHURA Ph.D.
Deputy Director,
Sea Fisheries Institute,
Gdynia

Mr Marek ZELAZKO
Legal Adviser,
Ministry for Foreign Trade and Marine Economy,
Warsaw

SOUTH AFRICA

Representative

Mr P.F. THERON
Secretary for Industries,
Pretoria

Alternate Representatives

Mr P.D. OELOFSEN
Senior Law Adviser,
Department of Foreign Affairs and Information,
Pretoria

Mr T.F. WHEELER
Under-Secretary,
Department of Foreign Affairs and Information
Pretoria

Mr G.H. STANDER
Director of Seafisheries,
Department of Agriculture and Fisheries,
Cape Town

Mr H.F. VAN ZYL
Third Secretary,
South African Embassy,
Canberra

U.S.S.R.

Representative

Dr Y.M. RYBAKOV
Head of Treaties and Legal Department,
Ministry of Foreign Affairs

Alternate Representatives

Dr V.V. GOLITSIN
Head of Division of Public International Law,
Treaties and Legal Department,
Ministry of Foreign Affairs

Dr T.G. LUBIMOVA
All Union Scientific Institute on Fishery
 and Oceanographic Research
Ministry of Fisheries

Dr V.K. ZILANOV
Deputy Head of Foreign Relations Department,
Ministry of Fisheries

Adviser

L.A. RAINA
Counsellor,
Embassy of the U.S.S.R.
Canberra

Secretary

Miss Ludmila P. PICHUGINA
Legal and Treaty Department,
Ministry of Foreign Affairs

UNITED KINGDOM

Representative

Sir Donald LOGAN K.C.M.G.
Foreign and Commonwealth Office
London

Alternate Representatives

Dr John A. HEAP
Head,
Polar Regions Section,
Foreign and Commonwealth Office,
London

Mr David EDWARDS
Legal Adviser,
Foreign and Commonwealth Office,
London

UNITED STATES

Representative

Morris D. BUSBY
Acting Deputy Assistant Secretary for
 Oceans and Fisheries Affairs,
Department of State

Alternate Representatives

R. TUCKER SCULLY
Acting Director,
Office of Oceans and Polar Affairs,
Department of State

Carmen J. BLONDIN
Director,
Office of International Fisheries Affairs,
National Marine Fisheries Service,
National Oceanic and Atmospheric Administration,
Department of Commerce

David COLSON
Office of the Legal Adviser
Department of State

Advisers

Joseph E. BENNETT
Division of Polar Programs,
National Science Foundation

Robert J. HOFMAN
Scientific Program Director,
Marine Mammal Commission

Alan F. RYAN
Foreign Affairs Officer,
Office of International Fisheries Affairs,
National Marine and Fisheries Service,
National Oceanic and Atmospheric Administration,
Department of Commerce

Private Sector Advisers

James N. BARNES
Center for Law and Social Policy,
Washington, D.C.

Katherine GREEN HAMMOND
Ecosystem Modeling and Simulation,
El Paso, Texas

        The following international organisations were invited by the
Government of Australia to participate as observers in the Conference
and appointed their delegations as follows:-

EUROPEAN COMMUNITIES

Representatives

Mr M. MARCUSSEN
Head of Division,
Commission of the European Communities

Professor J.H.J. BOURGEOIS
Legal Adviser,
Commission of the European Communities

Advisers

Representatives of the members of the Council of the European
Communities

Mr T.M. KASTEEL
Acting Representative of the Presidency of the Council of
  the European Communities,
Counsellor

Mr M. GORMSEN
First Secretary

General Secretariat of the Council of the European Communities

Professor Daniel VIGNES
Director, Legal Service

Mr Erik STEIN
Principal Administrator,
Directorate General of External Relations

Mrs M. GILOT-KOEHLER
Secretary

FOOD AND AGRICULTURE ORGANISATION

Mr Michel SAVINI
Regional Fisheries Law Adviser,
Fisheries Department

INTER-GOVERNMENTAL OCEANOGRAPHIC COMMISSION

Mr R.C. GRIFFITHS
Assistant Secretary

INTERNATIONAL UNION FOR THE CONSERVATION OF NATURE AND
NATURAL RESOURCES

Mr Robert BOOTE
Vice-President and Regional Councillor

Dr D.F. McMICHAEL
Treasurer and Regional Councillor

INTERNATIONAL WHALING COMMISSION

Professor J.D. OVINGTON
Australian Commissioner to the I.W.C.

SCIENTIFIC COMMITTEE ON ANTARCTIC RESEARCH

Dr David TRANTER
CSIRO
Division of Fisheries and Oceanography

SCIENTIFIC COMMITTEE ON OCEANIC RESEARCH

Dr G. HUMPHREY
University of Sydney

The Conference met at Canberra on 7 May 1980 under the Chairmanship of Mr J.E. Ryan, Representative of the delegation of Australia. The Secretary-General was Mr R.H. Wyndham.

A Drafting Committee established under the Rules of Procedure of the Conference was constituted as follows:

Mr David EDWARDS, United Kingdom   (Chairman)
His Excellency, Minister Ricardo Pedro QUADRI, Argentina
Senor Joaquin Daniel OTERO, Argentina
Mr John BAILEY, Australia
Senor Juan FONTECILLA, Chile
Senor Celso MORENO, Chile
Miss Josiane COURATIER, France
Mr Gerard BOIVINEAU, France
Mr Jun YOKOTA, Japan
Mr P.D. OELOFSEN, South Africa
Dr V.V. GOLITSIN, U.S.S.R.
Mr David COLSON, U.S.A.

The Final Session was held on 20 May 1980. As a result of its deliberations the Conference has established and drawn up for signature a "Convention of the Conservation of Antarctic Marine Living Resources" the text of which is annexed hereto.

The Conference also decided to include in the Final Act the text of the following statement made by the Chairman on 19 May 1980 regarding the application of the Convention on the Conservation of Antarctic Marine Living Resources to the waters adjacent to Kerguelen and Crozet over which France has jurisdiction and to waters adjacent to other islands within the area to which this Convention applies over which the existence of State sovereignty is recognized by all Contracting Parties.

"1. Measures for the conservation of Antarctic marine living resources of the waters adjacent to Kerguelen and Crozet, over which France has jurisdiction, adopted by France prior to the entry into force of the Convention, would remain in force after the entry into force of the Convention until modified by France acting within the framework of the Commission or otherwise.

2. After the Convention has come into force, each time the Commission should undertake examination of the conservation needs of the marine living resources of the general area in which the waters adjacent to Kerguelen and Crozet are to be found, it would be open to France either to agree that the waters in question should be included in the area of application of any specific conservation measure under consideration or to indicate that they should be excluded. In the latter event, the Commission would not proceed to the adoption of the specific conservation measure in a form applicable to the waters in question unless France removed its objection to it. France could also adopt such national measures as it might deem appropriate for the waters in question.

3. Accordingly, when specific conservation measures are considered within the framework of the Commission and with the participation of France, then:

(a) France would be bound by any conservation measures adopted by consensus with its participation for the duration of those measures. This would not prevent France from promulgating national measures that were more strict than the Commission's measures or which dealt with other matters;

(b) In the absence of consensus, France could promulgate any national measures which it might deem appropriate.

4. Conservation measures, whether national measures or measures adopted by the Commission, in respect of the waters adjacent to Kerguelen and Crozet, would be enforced by France. The system of observation and inspection foreseen by the Convention would not be implemented in the waters adjacent to Kerguelen and Crozet except as agreed by France and in the manner so agreed.

5. The understandings, set forth in paragraphs 1-4 above, regarding the application of the Convention to waters adjacent to the Islands of Kerguelen and Crozet, also apply to waters adjacent to the islands within the area

to which this Convention applies over which the existence
of State sovereignty is recognized by all Contracting Parties."

No objection to the statement was made.

II

The Conference on the Conservation of Antarctic Marine Living Resources,

Noting that a definitive regime for the conservation of Antarctic
marine living resources has been elaborated, and desiring to have that
regime enter into force as quickly as possible;

Recognizing that harvesting of Antarctic marine living resources is
presently taking place and underlining the importance of the
objectives of the Convention on the Conservation of Antarctic Marine
Living Resources;

Recognizing the need to identify, emphasize and co-operate in carrying
out research activities that will facilitate the effective operation
of the Convention;

Desiring further to facilitate the implementation of the Convention by
emphasizing and co-ordinating the collection of scientific and fisheries
data needed for the Scientific Committee to be constituted under the
terms of the Convention to begin effective work upon entry into force
of the Convention;

Calls upon the Parties entitled to become Members of the Commission

1. To take all possible steps to bring the Convention on the
    Conservation of Antarctic Marine Living Resources into
    force as soon as possible;

2. To show the greatest possible care and concern, bearing in
    mind the principles and objectives of Article II of the
    Convention, in any harvesting of Antarctic marine living resources
    in the period prior to entry into force of the Convention and
    examination of the status of stocks by the Scientific Committee
    to be established by the Convention on the Conservation of
    Antarctic Marine Living Resources;

3. To the greatest extent practicable and feasible to co-operate
    broadly and comprehensively in the continued development
    of the scientific and fisheries data necessary for the
    effective operation of the Convention on the Conservation
    of Antarctic Marine Living Resources, and to this end:

    (a) to intensify research related to Antarctic marine
         living resources;

    (b) to identify the specific scientific and fisheries
         data needed and how those data should be collected
         and recorded to facilitate the work of the Scientific

Committee to be established by the Convention; and

(c)   to compile scientific and fisheries data identified pursuant
      to sub-paragraph (b) above in order to distribute those
      data to the Contracting Parties upon entry into force of
      the Convention on the Conservation of Antarctic Marine
      Living Resources.

III

The Conference on the Convention for the Conservation of Antarctic
Marine Living Resources,

> Having agreed on a text of a Convention which
> would establish a Commission and Scientific
> Committee for the Conservation of Antarctic
> Marine Living Resources and an Executive
> Secretariat;
>
> Recognising the need to examine working methods
> for the Executive Secretary and Secretariat so
> that they may begin their work as soon as possible
> after entry into force of the Convention;

Takes note of the intention of the Depositary to convene a meeting of
representatives of Parties entitled to become Members of the Commission
within one year after expiration of the period during which the Convention
is open for signature for the purpose of considering steps which might
be taken to facilitate the early operation of the Commission,
Scientific Committee and Executive Secretariat when these bodies are
established.

IV

The Conference on the Conservation of Antarctic Marine Living Resources
resolves:

1.   to express its gratitude to the Australian Government for
     its initiative in convening the present Conference and
     for its preparation;

2.   to express to its Chairman, Mr J.E. Ryan, its deep
     appreciation for the admirable manner in which he has
     guided the Conference;

3.   to express to the officers and staff of the Secretariat
     its appreciation for their untiring efforts in
     contributing to the attainment of the objectives of
     the Conference.

<u>V</u>

The Conference on the Conservation of Antarctic Marine Living Resources resolves:

That the Government of Australia be authorised to publish the Final Act of this Conference and the text of the Convention annexed hereto.

<u>VI</u>

The Conference on the Conservation of Antarctic Marine Living Resources resolves:

To express its deep appreciation to the Australian Government for its offer to provide a site for the Headquarters of the Commission to be established under the Convention.

Done at Canberra, this Twentieth Day of May 1980, in a single original copy to be deposited in the archives of the Government of Australia which will transmit a certified copy thereof to all the other Participants in the Conference.

In witness whereof, the following representatives have signed this Final Act.

CONVENTION ON THE CONSERVATION OF ANTARCTIC MARINE LIVING RESOURCES

The Contracting Parties,

Recognising the importance of safeguarding the environment and protecting the integrity of the ecosystem of the seas surrounding Antarctica;

Noting the concentration of marine living resources found in Antarctic waters and the increased interest in the possibilities offered by the utilization of these resources as a source of protein;

Conscious of the urgency of ensuring the conservation of Antarctic marine living resources;

Considering that it is essential to increase knowledge of the Antarctic marine ecosystem and its components so as to be able to base decisions on harvesting on sound scientific information;

Believing that the conservation of Antarctic marine living resources calls for international co-operation with due regard for the provisions of the Antarctic Treaty and with the active involvement of all States engaged in research or harvesting activities in Antarctic waters;

Recognising the prime responsibilities of the Antarctic Treaty Consultative Parties for the protection and preservation of the Antarctic environment and, in particular, their responsibilities under Article IX, paragraph 1(f) of the Antarctic Treaty in respect of the preservation and conservation of living resources in Antarctica;

Recalling the action already taken by the Antarctic Treaty Consultative Parties including in particular the Agreed Measures for the Conservation of Antarctic Fauna and Flora, as well as the provisions of the Convention for the Conservation of Antarctic Seals;

Bearing in mind the concern regarding the conservation of Antarctic marine living resources expressed by the Consultative Parties at the Ninth Consultative Meeting of the Antarctic Treaty and the importance of the provisions of Recommendation IX-2 which led to the establishment of the present Convention;

Believing that it is in the interest of all mankind to preserve the waters surrounding the Antarctic continent for peaceful purposes only and to prevent their becoming the scene or object of international discord;

Recognising, in the light of the foregoing, that it is desirable to establish suitable machinery for recommending, promoting, deciding upon and co-ordinating the measures and scientific studies needed to ensure the conservation of Antarctic marine living organisms;

Have agreed as follows:

ARTICLE I

1.   This Convention applies to the Antarctic marine living resources of the area south of 60° South latitude and to the Antarctic marine living resources of the area between that latitude and the Antarctic Convergence which form part of the Antarctic marine ecosystem.

2.   Antarctic marine living resources means the populations of fin fish, molluscs, crustaceans and all other species of living organisms, including birds, found south of the Antarctic Convergence.

3.   The Antarctic marine ecosystem means the complex of relationships of Antarctic marine living resources with each other and with their physical environment.

4.   The Antarctic Convergence shall be deemed to be a line joining the following points along parallels of latitude and meridians of longitude:

50°S, 0°; 50°S, 30°E; 45°S, 30°E; 45°S, 80°E; 55°S, 80°E; 55°S, 150°E; 60°S, 150°E; 60°S, 50°W; 50°S, 50°W; 50°S, 0°.

ARTICLE II

1.   The objective of this Convention is the conservation of Antarctic marine living resources.

2.   For the purposes of this Convention, the term "conservation" includes rational use.

3.   Any harvesting and associated activities in the area to which this Convention applies shall be conducted in accordance with the provisions of this Convention and with the following principles of conservation:

(a)   prevention of decrease in the size of any harvested population to levels below those which ensure its stable recruitment. For this purpose its size should not be allowed to fall below a level close to that which ensures the greatest net annual increment;

(b)   maintenance of the ecological relationships between harvested, dependent and related populations of Antarctic marine living resources and the restoration of depleted populations to the levels defined in sub-paragraph (a) above; and

(c) prevention of changes or minimization of the risk of changes in the marine ecosystem which are not potentially reversible over two or three decades, taking into account the state of available knowledge of the direct and indirect impact of harvesting, the effect of the introduction of alien species, the effects of associated activities on the marine ecosystem and of the effects of environmental changes, with the aim of making possible the sustained conservation of Antarctic marine living resources.

ARTICLE III

The Contracting Parties, whether or not they are Parties to the Antarctic Treaty, agree that they will not engage in any activities in the Antarctic Treaty area contrary to the principles and purposes of that Treaty and that, in their relations with each other, they are bound by the obligations contained in Articles I and V of the Antarctic Treaty.

ARTICLE IV

1. With respect to the Antarctic Treaty area, all Contracting Parties, whether or not they are Parties to the Antarctic Treaty, are bound by Articles IV and VI of the Antarctic Treaty in their relations with each other.

2. Nothing in this Convention and no acts or activities taking place while the present Convention is in force shall:

(a) constitute a basis for asserting, supporting or denying a claim to territorial sovereignty in the Antarctic Treaty area or create any rights of sovereignty in the Antarctic Treaty area;

(b) be interpreted as a renunciation or diminution by any Contracting Party of, or as prejudicing, any right or claim or basis of claim to exercise coastal state jurisdiction under international law within the area to which this Convention applies;

(c) be interpreted as prejudicing the position of any Contracting Party as regards its recognition or non-recognition of any such right, claim or basis of claim;

(d) affect the provision of Article IV, paragraph 2, of the Antarctic Treaty that no new claim, or enlargement of an existing claim, to territorial sovereignty in Antarctica shall be asserted while the Antarctic Treaty is in force.

ARTICLE V

1.   The Contracting Parties which are not Parties to the Antarctic Treaty acknowledge the special obligations and responsibilities of the Antarctic Treaty Consultative Parties for the protection and preservation of the environment of the Antarctic Treaty area.

2.   The Contracting Parties which are not Parties to the Antarctic Treaty agree that, in their activities in the Antarctic Treaty area, they will observe as and when appropriate the Agreed Measures for the Conservation of Antarctic Fauna and Flora and such other measures as have been recommended by the Antarctic Treaty Consultative Parties in fulfilment of their responsibility for the protection of the Antarctic environment from all forms of harmful human interference.

3.   For the purposes of this Convention, "Antarctic Treaty Consultative Parties" means the Contracting Parties to the Antarctic Treaty whose Representatives participate in meetings under Article IX of the Antarctic Treaty.

ARTICLE VI

Nothing in this Convention shall derogate from the rights and obligations of Contracting Parties under the International Convention for the Regulation of Whaling and the Convention for the Conservation of Antarctic Seals.

ARTICLE VII

1.   The Contracting Parties hereby establish and agree to maintain the Commission for the Conservation of Antarctic Marine Living Resources (hereinafter referred to as "the Commission").

2.   Membership in the Commission shall be as follows:

(a)   each Contracting Party which participated in the meeting at which this Convention was adopted shall be a Member of the Commission;

(b)   each State Party which has acceded to this Convention pursuant to Article XXIX shall be entitled to be a Member of the Commission during such time as that acceding party is engaged in research or harvesting activities in relation to the marine living resources to which this Convention applies;

(c)   each regional economic integration organization which has acceded to this Convention pursuant to Article XXIX shall be entitled to be a Member of the Commission during such time as its States members are so entitled;

(d)   a Contracting Party seeking to participate in the work of the Commission pursuant to sub-paragraphs (b) and (c) above shall notify the Depositary of the basis upon which it seeks to become a Member of the Commission and of its willingness to accept conservation measures in force. The Depositary shall communicate to each member of the Commission such notification and accompanying information. Within two months of receipt of such communication from the Depositary, any Member of the Commission may request that a special meeting of the Commission beheld to consider the matter. Upon receipt of such request, the Depositary shall call such a meeting. If there is no request for a meeting, the Contracting Party submitting the notification shall be deemed to have satisfied the requirements for Commission Membership.

3.   Each Member of the Commission shall be represented by one representative who may be accompanied by alternate representatives and advisers.

ARTICLE VIII

The Commission shall have legal personality and shall enjoy in the territory of each of the States Parties such legal capacity as may be necessary to perform its function and achieve the purposes of this Convention. The privileges and immunities to be enjoyed by the Commission and its staff in the territory of a State Party shall be determined by agreement between the Commission and the State Party concerned.

ARTICLE IX

1.   The function of the Commission shall be to give effect to the objective and principles set out in Article II of this Convention. To this end, it shall:

(a)   facilitate research into and comprehensive studies of Antarctic marine living resources and of the Antarctic marine ecosystem;

(b)   compile data on the status of and changes in population of Antarctic marine living resources and on factors affecting the distribution, abundance and productivity of harvested species and dependent or related species or populations;

(c)   ensure the acquisition of catch and effort statistics on harvested populations;

(d)   analyse, disseminate and publish the information referred to in sub-paragraphs (b) and (c) above and the reports of the Scientific Committee;

(e)   identify conservation needs and analyse the effectiveness of conservation measures;

    (f)   formulate, adopt and revise conservation measures on the basis of the best scientific evidence available, subject to the provisions of paragraph 5 of this Article;

    (g)   implement the system of observation and inspection established under Article XXIV of this Convention;

    (h)   carry out such other activities as are necessary to fulfil the objective of this Convention.

2.   The conservation measures referred to in paragraph 1(f) above include the following:

    (a)   the designation of the quantity of any species which may be harvested in the area to which this Convention applies;

    (b)   the designation of regions and sub-regions based on the distribution of populations of Antarctic marine living resources;

    (c)   the designation of the quantity which may be harvested from the populations of regions and sub-regions;

    (d)   the designation of protected species;

    (e)   the designation of the size, age and, as appropriate, sex of species which may be harvested;

    (f)   the designation of open and closed seasons for harvesting;

    (g)   the designation of the opening and closing of areas, regions or sub-regions for purposes of scientific study or conservation, including special areas for protection and scientific study;

    (h)   regulation of the effort employed and methods of harvesting, including fishing gear, with a view, *inter alia*, to avoiding undue concentration of harvesting in any region or sub-region;

    (i)   the taking of such other conservation measures as the Commission considers necessary for the fulfilment of the objective of this Convention, including measures concerning the effects of harvesting and associated activities on components of the marine ecosystem other than the harvested populations.

3.   The Commission shall publish and maintain a record of all conservation measures in force.

4.   In exercising its functions under paragraph 1 above, the Commission shall take full account of the recommendations and advice of the Scientific Committee.

5.   The Commission shall take full account of any relevant measures or regulations established or recommended by the Consultative Meetings pursuant to Article IX of the Antarctic Treaty or by existing fisheries commissions responsible for species which may enter the area to which this Convention applies, in order that there shall be no inconsistency between the rights and obligations of a Contracting Party under

such regulations or measures and conservation measures which may be adopted by the Commission.

6. Conservation measures adopted by the Commission in accordance with this Convention shall be implemented by Members of the Commission in the following manner:

(a) the Commission shall notify conservation measures to all Members of the Commission;

(b) conservation measures shall become binding upon all Members of the Commission 180 days after such notification, except as provided in sub-paragraphs (c) and (d) below;

(c) if a Member of the Commission, within ninety days following the notification specified in sub-paragraph (a), notifies the Commission that it is unable to accept the conservation measure, in whole or in part, the measure shall not, to the extent stated, be binding upon that Member of the Commission;

(d) in the event that any Member of the Commission invokes the procedure set forth in sub-paragraph (c) above, the Commission shall meet at the request of any Member of the Commission to review the conservation measure. At the time of such meeting and within thirty days following the meeting, any Member of the Commission shall have the right to declare that it is no longer able to accept the conservation measure, in which case the Member shall no longer be bound by such measure.

ARTICLE X

1. The Commission shall draw the attention of any State which is not a Party to this Convention to any activity undertaken by its nationals or vessels which, in the opinion of the Commission, affects the implementation of the objective of this Convention.

2. The Commission shall draw the attention of all Contracting Parties to any activity which, in the opinion of the Commission, affects the implementation by a Contracting Party of the objective of this Convention or the compliance by that Contracting Party with its obligations under this Convention.

ARTICLE XI

The Commission shall seek to cooperate with Contracting Parties which may exercise jurisdiction in marine areas adjacent to the area to which this Convention applies in respect of the conservation of any stock or stocks of associated species which occur both within those areas and the area to which this Convention applies, with a view to harmonizing the conservation measures adopted in respect of such stocks.

ARTICLE XII

1.   Decisions of the Commission on matters of substance shall be taken by consensus. The question of whether a matter is one of substance shall be treated as a matter of substance.

2.   Decisions on matters other than those referred to in paragraph 1 above shall be taken by a simple majority of the Members of the Commission present and voting.

3.   In Commission consideration of any item requiring a decision, it shall be made clear whether a regional economic integration organization will participate in the taking of the decision and, if so, whether any of its member States will also participate. The number of Contracting Parties so participating shall not exceed the number of member States of the regional economic integration organization which are Members of the Commission.

4.   In the taking of decisions pursuant to this Article, a regional economic integration organization shall have only one vote.

ARTICLE XIII

1.   The headquarters of the Commission shall be established at Hobart, Tasmania, Australia.

2.   The Commission shall hold a regular annual meeting. Other meetings shall also be held at the request of one-third of its members and as otherwise provided in this Convention. The first meeting of the Commission shall be held within three months of the entry into force of this Convention, provided that among the Contracting Parties there are at least two States conducting harvesting activities within the area to which this Convention applies. The first meeting shall, in any event, be held within one year of the entry into force of this Convention. The Depositary shall consult with the signatory States regarding the first Commission meeting, taking into account that a broad representation of such States is necessary for the effective operation of the Commission.

3.   The Depositary shall convene the first meeting of the Commission at the headquarters of the Commission. Thereafter, meetings of the Commission shall be held at its headquarters, unless it decides otherwise.

4.   The Commission shall elect from among its members a Chairman and Vice-Chairman, each of whom shall serve for a term of two years and shall be eligible for re-election for one additional term. The first Chairman shall, however, be elected for

an initial term of three years. The Chairman and Vice-Chairman shall not be representatives of the same Contracting Party.

5.   The Commission shall adopt and amend as necessary the rules of procedure for the conduct of its meetings, except with respect to the matters dealt with in Article XII of this Convention.

6.   The Commission may establish such subsidiary bodies as are necessary for the performance of its functions.

ARTICLE XIV

1.   The Contracting Parties hereby establish the Scientific Committee for the Conservation of Antarctic Marine Living Resources (hereinafter referred to as "the Scientific Committee") which shall be a consultative body to the Commission. The Scientific Committee shall normally meet at the headquarters of the Commission unless the Scientific Committee decides otherwise.

2.   Each Member of the Commission shall be a member of the Scientific Committee and shall appoint a representative with suitable scientific qualifications who may be accompanied by other experts and advisers.

3.   The Scientific Committee may seek the advice of other scientists and experts as may be required on an ad hoc basis.

ARTICLE XV

1.   The Scientific Committee shall provide a forum for consultation and co-operation concerning the collection, study and exchange of information with respect to the marine living resources to which this Convention applies. It shall encourage and promote cooperation in the field of scientific research in order to extend knowledge of the marine living resources of the Antarctic marine ecosystem.

2.   The Scientific Committee shall conduct such activities as the Commission may direct in pursuance of the objective of this Convention and shall:

    (a)   establish criteria and methods to be used for determinations concerning the conservation measures referred to in Article IX of this Convention;

    (b)   regularly assess the status and trends of the populations of Antarctic marine living resources;

    (c)   analyse data concerning the direct and indirect effects of harvesting on the populations of Antarctic marine living resources;

    (d)   assess the effects of proposed changes in the methods or levels of harvesting and proposed conservation measures;

(e)   transmit assessments, analyses, reports and recommendations to the Commission as requested or on its own initiative regarding measures and research to implement the objective of this Convention;

(f)   formulate proposals for the conduct of international and national programs of research into Antarctic marine living resources.

3.   In carrying out its functions, the Scientific Committee shall have regard to the work of other relevant technical and scientific organizations and to the scientific activities conducted within the framework of the Antarctic Treaty.

ARTICLE XVI

1.   The first meeting of the Scientific Committee shall be held within three months of the first meeting of the Commission. The Scientific Committee shall meet thereafter as often as may be necessary to fulfil its functions.

2.   The Scientific Committee shall adopt and amend as necessary its rules of procedure. The rules and any amendments thereto shall be approved by the Commission. The rules shall include procedures for the presentation of minority reports.

3.   The Scientific Committee may establish, with the approval of the Commission, such subsidiary bodies as are necessary for the performance of its functions.

ARTICLE XVII

1.   The Commission shall appoint an Executive Secretary to serve the Commission and Scientific Committee according to such procedures and on such terms and conditions as the Commission may determine. His term of office shall be for four years and he shall be eligible for re-appointment.

2.   The Commission shall authorize such staff establishment for the Secretariat as may be necessary and the Executive Secretary shall appoint, direct and supervise such staff according to such rules and procedures and on such terms and conditions as the Commission may determine.

3.   The Executive Secretary and Secretariat shall perform the functions entrusted to them by the Commission.

ARTICLE XVIII

The official languages of the Commission and of the Scientific Committee shall be English, French, Russian and Spanish.

ARTICLE XIX

1.   At each annual meeting, the Commission shall adopt by consensus its budget and the budget of the Scientific Committee.

2.   The draft budget for the Commission and the Scientific Committee and any subsidiary bodies shall be prepared by the Executive Secretary and submitted to the Members of the Commission at least sixty days before the annual meeting of the Commission.

3.   Each Member of the Commission shall contribute to the budget. Until the expiration of five years after the entry into force of this Convention, the contribution of each Member of the Commission shall be equal. Thereafter the contribution shall be determined in accordance with two criteria: the amount harvested and an equal sharing among all Members of the Commission. The Commission shall determine by consensus the proportion in which these two criteria shall apply.

4.   The financial activities of the Commission and Scientific Committee shall be conducted in accordance with financial regulations adopted by the Commission and shall be subject to an annual audit by external auditors selected by the Commission.

5.   Each Member of the Commission shall meet its own expenses arising from attendance at meetings of the Commission and of the Scientific Committee.

6.   A Member of the Commission that fails to pay its contributions for two consecutive years shall not, during the period of its default, have the right to participate in the taking of decisions in the Commission.

ARTICLE XX

1.   The Members of the Commission shall, to the greatest extent possible, provide annually to the Commission and to the Scientific Committee such statistical, biological and other data and information as the Commission and Scientific Committee may require in the exercise of their functions.

2.   The Members of the Commission shall provide, in the manner and at such intervals as may be prescribed, information about their harvesting activities, including fishing areas and vessels, so as to enable reliable catch and effort statistics to be compiled.

3.   The Members of the Commission shall provide to the Commission at such intervals as may be prescribed information on steps taken to implement the conservation measures adopted by the Commission.

4.   The Members of the Commission agree that in any of their harvesting activities, advantage shall be taken of opportunities to collect data needed to assess the impact of harvesting.

ARTICLE XXI

1.   Each Contracting Party shall take appropriate measures within its competence to ensure compliance with the provisions of this Convention and with conservation measures adopted by the Commission to which the Party is bound in accordance with Article IX of this Convention.

2.   Each Contracting Party shall transmit to the Commission information on measures taken pursuant to paragraph 1 above, including the imposition of sanctions for any violation.

ARTICLE XXII

1.   Each Contracting Party undertakes to exert appropriate efforts, consistent with the Charter of the United Nations, to the end that no one engages in any activity contrary to the objective of this Convention.

2.   Each Contracting Party shall notify the Commission of any such activity which comes to its attention.

ARTICLE XXIII

1.   The Commission and the Scientific Committee shall co-operate with the Antarctic Treaty Consultative Parties on matters falling within the competence of the latter.

2.   The Commission and the Scientific Committee shall co-operate, as appropriate, with the Food and Agriculture Organisation of the United Nations and with other Specialised Agencies.

3.   The Commission and the Scientific Committee shall seek to develop co-operative working relationships, as appropriate, with inter-governmental and non-governmental organizations which could contribute to their work, including the Scientific Committee on Antarctic Research, the Scientific Committee on Oceanic Research and the International Whaling Commission.

4.   The Commission may enter into agreements with the organizations referred to in this Article and with other organizations as may be appropriate. The Commission and the Scientific Committee may invite such organizations to send observers to their meetings and to meetings of their subsidiary bodies.

ARTICLE XXIV

1.   In order to promote the objective and ensure observance of the provisions of this Convention, the Contracting Parties agree that a system of observation and inspection shall be established.

2.   The system of observation and inspection shall be elaborated by the Commission on the basis of the following principles:

(a)   Contracting Parties shall cooperate with each other to ensure the effective implementation of the system of observation and inspection, taking account of the existing international practice. This system shall include, *inter alia*, procedures for boarding and inspection by observers and inspectors designated by the Members of the Commission and procedures for flag state prosecution and sanctions on the basis of evidence resulting from such boarding and inspections. A report of such prosecutions and sanctions imposed shall be included in the information referred to in Article XXI of this Convention;

(b)   in order to verify compliance with measures adopted under this Convention, observation and inspection shall be carried out on board vessels engaged in scientific research or harvesting of marine living resources in the area to which this Convention applies, through observers and inspectors designated by the Members of the Commission and operating under terms and conditions to be established by the Commission;

(c)   designated observers and inspectors shall remain subject to the jurisdiction of the Contracting Party of which they are nationals. They shall report to the Member of the Commission by which they have been designated which in turn shall report to the Commission.

3.   Pending the establishment of the system of observation and inspection, the Members of the Commission shall seek to establish interim arrangements to designate observers and inspectors and such designated observers and inspectors shall be entitled to carry out inspections in accordance with the principles set out in paragraph 2 above.

ARTICLE XXV

1.   If any dispute arises between two or more of the Contracting Parties concerning the interpretation or application of this Convention, those Contracting Parties shall consult among themselves with a view to having the dispute resolved by negotiation, inquiry, mediation, conciliation, arbitration, judicial settlement or other peaceful means of their own choice.

2.   Any dispute of this character not so resolved shall, with the consent in each case of all Parties to the dispute, be referred for settlement to the International Court of Justice or to arbitration; but failure to reach agreement on reference to the International Court or to arbitration shall not absolve Parties to the dispute from the responsibility of continuing to seek to resolve it by any of the various peaceful means referred to in paragraph 1 above.

3.   In cases where the dispute is referred to arbitration, the arbitral tribunal shall be constituted as provided in the Annex to this Convention.

ARTICLE XXVI

1.   This Convention shall be open for signature at Canberra from 1 August to 31 December 1980 by the States participating in the Conference on the Conservation of Antarctic Marine Living Resources held at Canberra from 7 to 20 May 1980.

2.   The States which so sign will be the original signatory States of the Convention.

ARTICLE XXVII

1.   This Convention is subject to ratification, acceptance or approval by signatory States.

2.   Instruments of ratification, acceptance or approval shall be deposited with the Government of Australia, hereby designated as the Depositary.

ARTICLE XXVIII

1.   This Convention shall enter into force on the thirtieth day following the date of deposit of the eighth instrument of ratification, acceptance or approval by States referred to in paragraph 1 of Article XXVI of this Convention.

2.   With respect to each State or regional economic integration organization which subsequent to the date of entry into force of this Convention deposits an instrument of ratification, acceptance, approval or accession, the Convention shall enter into force on the thirtieth day following such deposit.

ARTICLE XXIX

1.   This Convention shall be open for accession by any State interested in research or harvesting activities in relation to the marine living resources to which this Convention applies.

2. This Convention shall be open for accession by regional economic integration organizations constituted by sovereign States which include among their members one or more States Members of the Commission and to which the States members of the organization have transferred, in whole or in part, competences with regard to the matters covered by this Convention. The accession of such regional economic integration organizations shall be the subject of consultations among Members of the Commission.

ARTICLE XXX

1. This Convention may be amended at any time.

2. If one-third of the Members of the Commission request a meeting to discuss a proposed amendment the Depositary shall call such a meeting.

3. An amendment shall enter into force when the Depositary has received instruments of ratification, acceptance or approval thereof from all the Members of the Commission.

4. Such amendment shall thereafter enter into force as to any other Contracting Party when notice of ratification, acceptance or approval by it has been received by the Depositary. Any such Contracting Party from which no such notice has been received within a period of one year from the date of entry into force of the amendment in accordance with paragraph 3 above shall be deemed to have withdrawn from this Convention.

ARTICLE XXXI

1. Any Contracting Party may withdraw from this Convention on 30 June of any year, by giving written notice no later than 1 January of the same year to the Depositary, which, upon receipt of such a notice, shall communicate it forthwith to the other Contracting Parties.

2. Any other Contracting Party may, within sixty days of the receipt of a copy of such a notice from the Depositary, give written notice of withdrawal to the Depositary in which case the Convention shall cease to be in force on 30 June of the same year with respect to the Contracting Party giving such notice.

3. Withdrawal from this Convention by any Member of the Commission shall not affect its financial obligations under this Convention.

ARTICLE XXXII

The Depositary shall notify all Contracting Parties of the following:

(a) signatures of this Convention and the deposit of instruments of ratification, acceptance, approval or accession;

(b) the date of entry into force of this Convention and of any amendment thereto.

ARTICLE XXXIII

1.   This Convention, of which the English, French, Russian and Spanish texts are equally authentic, shall be deposited with the Government of Australia which shall transmit duly certified copies thereof to all signatory and acceding Parties.

2.   This Convention shall be registered by the Depositary pursuant to Article 102 of the Charter of the United Nations.

Drawn up at Canberra this twentieth day of May 1980.

IN WITNESS WHEREOF the undersigned, being duly authorized, have signed this Convention.

ANNEX FOR AN ARBITRAL TRIBUNAL

The arbitral tribunal referred to in paragraph 3 of Article XXV shall be composed of three arbitrators who shall be appointed as follows:

The Party commencing proceedings shall communicate the name of an arbitrator to the other Party which, in turn, within a period of forty days following such notification, shall communicate the name of the second arbitrator. The Parties shall, within a period of sixty days following the appointment of the second arbitrator, appoint the third arbitrator, who shall not be a national of either Party and shall not be of the same nationality as either of the first two arbitrators. The third arbitrator shall preside over the tribunal.

If the second arbitrator has not been appointed within the prescribed period, or if the Parties have not reached agreement within the prescribed period on the appointment of the third arbitrator, that arbitrator shall be appointed, as the request of either Party, by the Secretary-General of the Permanent Court of Arbitration, from among persons of international standing not having the nationality of a State which is a Party to this Convention.

The arbitral tribunal shall decide where its headquarters will be located and shall adopt its own rules of procedure.

The award of the arbitral tribunal shall be made by a majority of its members, who may not abstain from voting.

Any Contracting Party which is not a Party to the dispute may intervene in the proceedings with the consent of the arbitral tribunal.

The award of the arbitral tribunal shall be final and binding on all Parties to the dispute and on any Party which intervenes in the proceedings and shall be complied with without delay. The arbitral tribunal shall interpret the award at the request of one of the Parties to the dispute or of any intervening Party.

Unless the arbitral tribunal determines otherwise because of the particular circumstances of the case, the expenses of the tribunal, including the remuneration of its members, shall be borne by the Parties to the dispute in equal shares.

CONVENTION FOR THE CONSERVATION OF ANTARCTIC SEALS (CCAS)

CONVENTION
FOR THE CONSERVATION OF ANTARCTIC SEALS

The Contracting Parties,

Recalling the Agreed Measures for the Conservation of Antarctic Fauna and Flora, adopted under the Antarctic Treaty signed at Washington on 1 December 1959;

Recognizing the general concern about the vulnerability of Antarctic seals to commercial exploitation and the consequent need for effective conservation measures;

Recognizing that the stocks of Antarctic seals are an important living resource in the marine environment which requires an international agreement for its effective conservation;

Recognizing that this resource should not be depleted by over-exploitation, and hence that any harvesting should be regulated so as not to exceed the levels of the optimum sustainable yield;

Recognizing that in order to improve scientific knowledge and so place exploitation on a rational basis, every effort should be made both to encourage biological and other research on Antarctic seal populations and to gain information from such research and from the statistics of future sealing operations, so that further suitable regulations may be formulated;

Noting that the Scientific Committee on Antarctic Research of the International Council of Scientific Unions (SCAR) is willing to carry out the tasks requested of it in this Convention;

Desiring to promote and achieve the objectives of protection, scientific study and rational use of Antarctic seals, and to maintain a satisfactory balance within the ecological system,

Have agreed as follows:

ARTICLE I
SCOPE

1.   This Convention applies to the seas south of 60° South Latitude, in respect of which the Contracting Parties affirm the provisions of Article IV of the Antarctic Treaty.

2.   This Convention may be applicable to any or all of the following species:

Southern elephant seal *Mirounga leonina,*

Leopard seal *Hydrurga leptonyx,*

Weddell seal *Leptonychotes weddelli,*

Crabeater seal *Lobodon carcinophagus,*

Ross seal *Ommatophoca rossi,*

Southern fur seals *Arctocephalus sp.*

3.   The Annex to this Convention forms an integral part thereof.

ARTICLE 2
IMPLEMENTATION

1.   The Contracting Parties agree that the species of seals enumerated in Article 1 shall not be killed or captured within the Convention area by their nationals or vessels under their respective flags except in accordance with the provisions of this Convention.

2   Each Contracting Party shall adopt for its nationals and for vessels under its flag such laws, regulations and other measures, including a permit system as appropriate, as may be necessary to implement this Convention.

ARTICLE 3
ANNEXED MEASURES

1.   This Convention includes an Annex specifying measures which the Contracting Parties hereby adopt. Contracting Parties may from time to time in the future adopt other measures with respect to the conservation, scientific study and rational and humane use of seal resources, prescribing *inter alia*:

(a)   permissible catch;

(b)   protected and unprotected species;

(c)   open and closed seasons;

(d)   open and closed areas, including the designation of reserves;

(e)   the designation of special areas where there shall be no disturbance of seals;

(f)   limits relating to sex, size, or age for each species;

(g)   restrictions relating to time of day and duration, limitations of effort and methods of sealing;

(h)   types and specifications of gear and apparatus and appliances which may be used;

(i)   catch returns and other statistical and biological records;

(j)   procedures for facilitating the review and assessment of scientific information;

(k)   other regulatory measures including an effective system of inspection.

2.   The measures adopted under paragraph (1) of this Article shall be based upon the best scientific and technical evidence available.

3.   The Annex may from time to time be amended in accordance with the procedures provided for in Article 9.

ARTICLE 4
SPECIAL PERMITS

1.   Notwithstanding the provisions of this Convention, any Contracting Party may issue permits to kill or capture seals in limited quantities and in conformity with the objectives and principles of this Convention for the following purposes:

(a)   to provide indispensable food for men or dogs;

(b)   to provide for scientific research; or

(c)   to provide specimens for museums, educational or cultural institutions.

2.   Each Contracting Party shall, as soon as possible, inform the other Contracting Parties and SCAR of the purpose and content of all permits issued under paragraph (1) of this Article and subsequently of the numbers of seals killed or captured under these permits.

ARTICLE 5
EXCHANGE OF INFORMATION AND SCIENTIFIC ADVICE

1.   Each Contracting Party shall provide to the other Contracting Parties and to SCAR the information specified in the Annex within the period indicated therein.

2.   Each Contracting Party shall also provide to the other Contracting Parties and to SCAR before 31 October each year information on any steps it has taken in accordance with Article 2 of this Convention during the preceding period 1 July to 30 June.

3.   Contracting Parties which have no information to report under the two preceding paragraphs shall indicate this formally before 31 October each year.

4.   SCAR is invited:

    (a)   to assess information received pursuant to this Article; encourage exchange of scientific data and information among the Contracting Parties; recommend programmes for scientific research; recommend statistical and biological data to be collected by sealing expeditions within the Convention area; and suggest amendments to the Annex; and

    (b)   to report on the basis of the statistical, biological and other evidence available when the harvest of any species of seal in the Convention area is having a significantly harmful effect on the total stocks of such species or on the ecological system in any particular locality.

5.   SCAR is invited to notify the Depositary which shall report to the Contracting Parties when SCAR estimates in any sealing season that the permissible catch limits for any species are likely to be exceeded and, in that case, to provide an estimate of the date upon which the permissible catch limits will be reached. Each Contracting Party shall then take appropriate measures to prevent its nationals and vessels under its flag from killing or capturing seals of that species after the estimated date until the Contracting Parties decide otherwise.

6.   SCAR may if necessary seek the technical assistance of the Food and Agriculture Organization of the United Nations in making its assessments.

7.   Notwithstanding the provisions of paragraph (1) of Article 1 the Contracting Parties shall, in accordance with their internal law, report to each other and to SCAR, for consideration, statistics relating to the Antarctic seals listed in paragraph (2) of Article 1 which have been killed or captured by their nationals and vessels under their respective flags in the area of floating sea ice north of 60° South Latitude.

ARTICLE 6

CONSULTATIONS BETWEEN CONTRACTING PARTIES

1.   At any time after commercial sealing has begun a Contracting Party may propose through the Depositary that a meeting of Contracting Parties be convened with a view to:

    (a)   establishing by a two-thirds majority of the Contracting Parties, including the concurring votes of all States signatory to this Convention present at the meeting, an effective system of control, including inspection, over the implementation of the provisions of this Convention;

(b)   establishing a commission to perform such functions under this Convention as the Contracting Parties may deem necessary; or

(c)   considering other proposals, including:

    (i)   the provision of independent scientific advice;

    (ii)   the establishment, by a two-thirds majority, of a scientific advisory committee which may be assigned some or all of the functions requested of SCAR under this Convention, if commercial sealing reaches significant proportions;

    (iii)   the carrying out of scientific programmes with the participation of the Contracting Parties; and

    (iv)   the provision of further regulatory measures, including moratoria.

2.   If one-third of the Contracting Parties indicate agreement the Depositary shall convene such a meeting, as soon as possible.

3.   A meeting shall be held at the request of any Contracting Party, if SCAR reports that the harvest of any species of Antarctic seal in the area to which this Convention applies is having a significantly harmful effect on the total stocks or the ecological system in any particular locality.

ARTICLE 7
REVIEW OF OPERATIONS

The Contracting Parties shall meet within five years after the entry into force of this Convention and at least every five years thereafter to review the operation of the Convention.

ARTICLE 8
AMENDMENTS TO THE CONVENTION

1.   This Convention may be amended at any time. The text of any amendment proposed by a Contracting Party shall be submitted to the Depositary, which shall transmit it to all the Contracting Parties.

2.   If one-third of the Contracting Parties request a meeting to discuss the proposed amendment the Depositary shall call such a meeting.

3.   An amendment shall enter into force when the Depositary has received instruments of ratification or acceptance thereof from all the Contracting Parties.

ARTICLE 9

AMENDMENTS TO THE ANNEX

1.   Any Contracting Party may propose amendments to the Annex to this Convention. The text of any such proposed amendment shall be submitted to the Depositary which shall transmit it to all Contracting Parties.

2.   Each such proposed amendment shall become effective for all Contracting Parties six months after the date appearing on the notification from the Depositary to the Contracting Parties, if within 120 days of the notification date, no objection has been received and two-thirds of the Contracting Parties have notified the Depositary in writing of their approval.

3.   If an objection is received from any Contracting Party within 120 days of the notification date, the matter shall be considered by the Contracting Parties at their next meeting. If unanimity on the matter is not reached at the meeting, the Contracting Parties shall notify the Depositary within 120 days from the date of closure of the meeting of their approval or rejection of the original amendment or of any new amendment proposed by the meeting. If, by the end of this period, two-thirds of the Contracting Parties have approved such amendment, it shall become effective six months from the date of the closure of the meeting for those Contracting Parties which have by then notified their approval.

4.   Any Contracting Party which has objected to a proposed amendment may at any time withdraw that objection, and the proposed amendment shall become effective with respect to such Party immediately if the amendment is already in effect, or at such time as it becomes effective under the terms of this Article.

5.   The Depositary shall notify each Contracting Party immediately upon receipt of each approval or objection, of each withdrawal of objection, and of the entry into force of any amendment.

6.   Any State which becomes a Party to this Convention after an amendment to the Annex has entered into force shall be bound by the Annex as so amended. Any State which becomes a Party to this Convention during the period when a proposed amendment is pending may approve or object to such an amendment within the time limits applicable to other Contracting Parties.

ARTICLE 10

SIGNATURE

This Convention shall be open for signature at London from 1 June to 31 December 1972 by States participating in the Conference on the Conservation of Antarctic Seals held at London from 3 to 11 February 1972.

ARTICLE 11

RATIFICATION

This Convention is subject to ratification or acceptance. Instruments of ratification or acceptance shall be deposited with the Government of the United Kingdom of Great Britain and Northern Ireland, hereby designated as the Depositary.

ARTICLE 12

ACCESSION

This Convention shall be open for accession by any State which may be invited to accede to this Convention with the consent of all the Contracting Parties.

ARTICLE 13

ENTRY INTO FORCE

1.   This Convention shall enter into force on the thirtieth day following the date of deposit of the seventh instrument of ratification or acceptance.

2.   Thereafter this Convention shall enter into force for each ratifying, accepting or acceding State on the thirtieth day after deposit by such State of its instrument of ratification, acceptance or accession.

ARTICLE 14

WITHDRAWAL

Any Contracting Party may withdraw from this Convention on 30 June of any year by giving notice on or before 1 January of the same year to the Depositary, which upon receipt of such a notice shall at once communicate it to the other Contracting Parties. Any other Contracting Party may, in like manner, within one month of the receipt of a copy of such a notice from the Depositary, give notice of withdrawal, so that the Convention shall cease to be in force on 30 June of the same year with respect to the Contracting Party giving such notice.

ARTICLE 15

NOTIFICATIONS BY THE DEPOSITARY

The Depositary shall notify all signatory and acceding States of the following:

(a) signatures of this Convention, the deposit of instruments of ratification, acceptance or accession and notices of withdrawal;

(b) the date of entry into force of this Convention and of any amendments to it or its Annex.

ARTICLE 16

CERTIFIED COPIES AND REGISTRATION

1. This Convention, done in the English, French, Russian and Spanish languages, each version being equally authentic, shall be deposited in the archives of the Government of the United Kingdom of Great Britain and Northern Ireland, which shall transmit duly certified copies thereof to all signatory and acceding States.

2. This Convention shall be registered by the Depositary pursuant to Article 102 of the Charter of the United Nations.

IN WITNESS WHEREOF, the undersigned, duly authorized, have signed this Convention.

DONE at London, this 1st day of June 1972.

ANNEX[1]

1. *PERMISSIBLE CATCH*

The Contracting Parties shall in any one year, which shall run from 1 March to the last day in February inclusive, restrict the total number of seals of each species killed or captured to the numbers specified below. These numbers are subject to review in the light of scientific assessments:

(a)   in the case of Crabeater seals *Lobodon carcinophagus*, 175,000;

(b)   in the case of Leopard seals *Hydrurga leptonyx*, 12,000;

(c)   in the case of Weddell seals *Leptonychotes weddelli*, 5,000.

2. *PROTECTED SPECIES*

(a)   It is forbidden to kill or capture Ross seals *Ommatophoca rossi*, Southern elephant seals *Mirounga leonina*, or fur seals of the genus *Arctocephalus*.

(b)   In order to protect the adult breeding stock during the period when it is most concentrated and vulnerable, it is forbidden to kill or capture any Weddell seal *Leptonychotes weddelli* between 1 September and 31 January inclusive.

3. *CLOSED SEASON AND SEALING SEASON*

The period between 1 March and 31 August inclusive is a Closed Season, during which the killing or capturing of seals is forbidden. The period 1 September to the last day in February constitutes a Sealing Season.

4. *SEALING ZONES*

Each of the sealing zones listed in this paragraph shall be closed in numerical sequence to all sealing operations for the seal species listed in paragraph 1 of this Annex for the period 1 September to the last day of February inclusive. Such closures shall begin with the same zone as is closed under paragraph 2 of Annex B to Annex 1 of the Report of the Fifth Antarctic Treaty Consultative Meeting at the moment the Convention enters into force. Upon the expiration of each closed period, the affected zone shall reopen:

Zone 1 – between 60° and 120° West Longitude.

---

[1] Text as amended in the CCAS Review Meeting (London, 12-16 September 1988). The amendments became effective on 27 March 1990.

Zone 2 – between 0° and 60° West Longitude, together with that part of the Weddell Sea lying westward of 60° West Longitude.

Zone 3 – between 0° and 70° East Longitude.

Zone 4 – between 70° and 130° East Longitude.

Zone 5 – between 130° East Longitude and 170° West Longitude.

Zone 6 – between 120° and 170° West Longitude.

5. SEAL RESERVES

It is forbidden to kill or capture seals in the following reserves, which are seal breeding areas or the site of long-term scientific research:

(a) The area around the South Orkney Islands between 60°20' and 60°56' South Latitude and 44°05' and 46°25' West Longitude.

(b) The area of the southwestern Ross Sea south of 76° South Latitude and west of 170° East Longitude.

(c) The area of Edisto Inlet south and west of a line drawn between Cape Hallett at 72°19' South Latitude, 170°18' East Longitude, and Helm Point, at 72°11' South Latitude, 170°00' East Longitude.

6. EXCHANGE OF INFORMATION

(a) Contracting Parties shall provide before 30 June each year to other Contracting Parties and to SCAR a summary of statistical information on all seals killed or captured by their nationals and vessels under their respective flags in the Convention area, in respect of the preceding period 1 March to the last day in February. This information shall include by zones and months:

(i) The gross and nett tonnage, brake horse-power, number of crew, and number of days' operation of vessels under the flag of the Contracting Party;

(ii) The number of adult individuals and pups of each species taken.

When specially requested, this information shall be provided in respect of each ship, together with its daily position at noon each operating day and the catch on that day.

(b) When an industry has started, reports of the number of seals of each species killed or captured in each zone shall be made to SCAR in the form and at the intervals (not shorter than one week) requested by that body.

(c) Contracting Parties shall provide to SCAR biological information, in particular:

(i)   Sex.

(ii) Reproductive condition.

(iii) Age.

SCAR may request additional information or material with the approval of the Contracting Parties.

(d) Contracting Parties shall provide to other Contracting Parties and to SCAR at least 30 days in advance of departure from their home ports, information on proposed sealing expeditions.

7. SEALING METHODS

(a) SCAR is invited to report on methods of sealing and to make recommendations with a view to ensuring that the killing or capturing of seals is quick, painless and efficient. Contracting Parties, as appropriate, shall adopt rules for their nationals and vessels under their respective flags engaged in the killing and capturing of seals, giving due consideration to the views of SCAR.

(b) In the light of the available scientific and technical data, Contracting Parties agree to take appropriate steps to ensure that their nationals and vessels under their respective flags refrain from killing or capturing seals in the water, except in limited quantities to provide for scientific research in conformity with the objectives and principles of this Convention. Such research shall include studies as to the effectiveness of methods of sealing from the viewpoint of the management and humane and rational utilization of the Antarctic seal resources for conservation purposes. The undertaking and the results of any such scientific research programme shall be communicated to SCAR and the Depositary which shall transmit them to the Contracting Parties.

8. COOPERATION

The Contracting Parties to this Convention shall, as appropriate, cooperate and exchange information with the other Contracting Parties to the other international instruments within the Antarctic Treaty System and their respective institutions.

SPECIAL PERMITS FOR THE KILLING
OR CAPTURING OF SEALS

The Meeting agreed:

A.   When considering the issue of a special permit, each Contracting Party should:

(a)   ensure that the number of seals permitted to be killed or captured is strictly limited to the minimum necessary to meet the purpose for which the permit is sought;

(b)   or permits for scientific research, take all feasible steps to encourage co-operative planning and to minimise wasteful duplication; and, for all permits, take all feasible steps to maximise the scientific benefits derived. To these ends, permits should be issued as far in advance as possible of the commencement of activity under the permit.

B.   Contracting Parties should provide to other Contracting Parties and SCAR the following information in respect of each permit:

(a)   without delay after a permit is issued:

(i)   the purpose of the permit, including the specific objectives of the research for which a scientific research permit is being issued;

(ii)   the content of the permit including the locality, time period, number, species and relative age of seals permitted to be killed or captured;

(b)   annually, by 30 June, a report describing activities undertaken under special permits in the previous year, including, as appropriate, the following information for each seal killed or captured:

(i)   Specimen number.

(ii)   Species.

(iii) Collection date.

(iv)   Collection location.

(v)   Sex.

(vi)   Relative age or size.

(vii) Reproductive condition (immature, mature, pregnant, lactating).

(viii) Type of specimen material collected (e.g. teeth, reproductive organs, skeletal material, stomach contents, tissue samples, blood, urine, organs, etc.).

[Paragraph 17 of the Final Report of the 1988 Meeting to Review the Operation of the Convention for the Conservation of Antarctic Seals.]

SECRETARIAT

HEADQUARTERS AGREEMENT
FOR THE SECRETARIAT OF THE ANTARCTIC TREATY

The Antarctic Treaty Consultative Meeting (ATCM) and the Argentine Republic,

Convinced of the need to strengthen the Antarctic Treaty system;

Bearing in mind the special legal and political status of Antarctica and the special responsibility of the Antarctic Treaty Consultative Parties to ensure that all activities in Antarctica are consistent with the purposes and principles of the Antarctic Treaty and its Protocol on Environmental Protection;

Having regard to Decision 1 (2001) of the XXIV ATCM and Measure 1 (2003) of the XXVI ATCM on the Secretariat of the Antarctic Treaty in Buenos Aires, Argentina;

Desiring to enable the Secretariat as an organ of the ATCM fully and efficiently to fulfill its purposes and functions; and

Desiring to define the legal capacity of the Secretariat as an organ of the ATCM as well as its privileges and immunities and those of the Executive Secretary and other staff members in the territory of the Argentine Republic;

Have agreed as follows:

ARTICLE 1
DEFINITIONS

For the purpose of this Agreement:

(a) "Antarctic Treaty" or "the Treaty" means the Antarctic Treaty done at Washington on 1 December 1959;

(b) "Appropriate Authorities" means the national, provincial or local authorities of the Argentine Republic in accordance with the laws of the Argentine Republic;

(c) "Archives" means all correspondence, documents, manuscripts, photographs, computer data storage, films, recordings and any other records, in paper, electronic or any other form, belonging to or held by the Secretariat;

(d) "Committee for Environmental Protection" or "CEP" means the Committee established under Article 11 of the Protocol;

(e) "Delegates" means Representatives, Alternate Representatives, Advisers and any other persons who represent the States Parties;

(f) "Executive Secretary" means the Executive Secretary appointed by the ATCM to head the Secretariat according to the instrument establishing the Secretariat;

(g) "Expert" means a person engaged to perform short term or temporary projects on behalf of the Secretariat or participate in the work of or perform a mission on behalf of the Secretariat without necessarily receiving remuneration from the Secretariat, but does not include staff members;

(h) "Government" means the Government of the Argentine Republic;

(i) "Headquarters" means the premises, including buildings or parts of buildings and any land ancillary thereto, irrespective of ownership, occupied by the Secretariat for the performance of its Official Activities;

(j) "Official Activities" means all activities undertaken pursuant to the Treaty and the Protocol including the Secretariat's administrative activities;

(k) "Protocol" means the Protocol on Environmental Protection to the Antarctic Treaty done at Madrid on 4 October 1991;

(l) "Secretariat" means the Secretariat of the Antarctic Treaty, established as a permanent organ of the ATCM;

(m) "Staff member" means the Executive Secretary and all other persons appointed for employment with the Secretariat and subject to its Staff Regulations, but does not include persons recruited locally and assigned to hourly rates of pay; and

(n) "States Parties" means the States Parties to the Antarctic Treaty.

ARTICLE 2

LEGAL CAPACITY

The Secretariat as an organ of the ATCM has legal personality and capacity to perform its functions in the territory of the Argentine Republic. It has, in particular, the capacity to contract, to acquire and dispose of movable and immovable property, and to institute and be a party to legal proceedings. The Secretariat may exercise its legal capacity only to the extent authorized by the ATCM.

ARTICLE 3

HEADQUARTERS

1. The Headquarters shall be inviolable and shall be under the full authority of the Secretariat.

2.   The Government shall provide premises rent-free, in Buenos Aires, suitable as the Headquarters.

3.   The Government shall take all appropriate steps to protect the Headquarters against any intrusion or damage and to prevent any impairment of its dignity.

4.   The Government shall arrange for the Headquarters to be supplied by the appropriate authorities with available public services, such as electricity, water, sewerage, gas, mail, telephone, telegraph, drainage, garbage collection and fire protection, on terms no less favourable than those enjoyed by diplomatic missions in Argentine Republic.

5.   Through the ATCM, the Secretariat shall make known to the Government the need for any changes to the location or extent of its permanent premises or archives and of any temporary occupation of premises for the performance of its Official Activities. Where any premises other than those provided under paragraph 2 above are used or occupied by the Secretariat for the performance of its Official Activities, such premises shall, with the concurrence of the Government, be accorded the status of official premises of the Secretariat. Where any permanent or temporary changes are made to the premises of the Secretariat in accordance with this paragraph, any additional premises occupied by the Secretariat shall not necessarily be provided by the Government rent-free.

6.   Without prejudice to the terms of this Agreement, the Secretariat shall not permit the Headquarters to become a refuge from justice for persons avoiding arrest or service of legal process or against whom an order of extradition or deportation has been issued.

7.   The Appropriate Authorities may enter the Headquarters to carry out their duties only with the consent of the Executive Secretary and under the conditions agreed by him/her. The Executive Secretary's consent shall be deemed to have been given in the case of fire or other exceptional emergencies which require immediate protective action.

ARTICLE 4
IMMUNITIES

1.   Subject to what is provided for in the Treaty, the Protocol or this Agreement, the activities of the Secretariat in the Argentine Republic shall be governed by Argentine domestic law consistent with international law.

2.   Within the scope of its Official Activities, the Secretariat as an organ of the ATCM and its property, premises and assets shall have immunity of jurisdiction in judicial and administrative proceedings except:

(a) to the extent that the ATCM expressly waives such immunity;

(b) in respect of any contract for the supply of goods or services and any loan or other transaction for the provision of finance and any guarantee or indemnity in respect of any such transaction or of any other financial obligation;

(c) in respect of a civil action by a third party for death, damage or personal injury arising from an accident caused by a motor vehicle belonging to, or operated on behalf of, the Secretariat to the extent that compensation is not recoverable from insurance;

(d) in respect of a motor vehicle offence involving a motor vehicle belonging to, or operated on behalf of, the Secretariat;

(e) in the event of a claim for salaries, wages or other emoluments owed by the Secretariat;

(f) in respect of a counter-claim directly connected with proceedings initiated by the Secretariat;

(g) in respect of claims made on real estate situated in the Argentine Republic; and

(h) in respect of actions based on the Secretariat's status as heir or beneficiary of property situated in the Argentine Republic.

3. The Secretariat's property, premises and assets shall have immunity from any form of restrictions or controls such as requisition, confiscation, expropriation or attachment. They shall also be immune from any form of administrative or judicial constraint provided that motor vehicles belonging to or operated on behalf of the Secretariat shall not be immune from administrative or judicial constraint when temporarily necessary in connection with the prevention of, and investigation into, accidents involving such motor vehicles.

4. Nothing in this Agreement shall impair, or shall be construed as a waiver of, immunity that States enjoy in the territory of other States.

ARTICLE 5
OBJECTIVE AND WAIVER OF PRIVILEGES AND IMMUNITIES

1. Privileges and immunities provided for in this Agreement are granted to ensure the unimpeded functioning of the ATCM and the Secretariat and the complete independence of the persons to whom they are accorded. They are not granted for the personal benefit of the individuals themselves.

2. Except as provided in paragraph 3 below, the privileges and immunities provided in this Agreement may be waived by the ATCM. They should be waived in

a particular case where the privilege and immunity in question would impede the course of justice and can be waived without prejudice to the purpose for which they are accorded.

3. In the case of Delegates, their privileges and immunities provided in this Agreement may be waived by the States Parties which they respectively represent.

ARTICLE 6
ARCHIVES

The Archives shall be inviolable.

ARTICLE 7
THE TREATY FLAG AND EMBLEM

The Secretariat shall be entitled to display the Treaty flag and emblem on the premises and means of transport of the Secretariat and of the Executive Secretary.

ARTICLE 8
EXEMPTION FROM DIRECT TAXES

Within the scope of its Official Activities, the Secretariat, its property, premises and assets, and its income (including contributions made to the Secretariat as the result of any agreement arrived at by the States Parties) shall be exempt from all direct taxes including income tax, capital gains tax and all State taxes. The Secretariat shall be exempt from municipal taxes with the exception of those which constitute payment for specific services rendered in accordance with paragraph 4 of Article 3 above.

ARTICLE 9
EXEMPTION FROM CUSTOMS AND EXCISE DUTIES AND VALUE ADDED TAX

1. The property used by the Secretariat necessary for its Official Activities (including the ATCM publications, motor vehicles and items for official entertainment purposes) shall be exempt from all customs and excise duties.

2. The Secretariat shall be exempt from any value added tax or similar taxes for services and goods, including publications and other information material, motor vehicles and items for official entertainment purposes, if the services and goods so purchased by the Secretariat are necessary for its official use.

ARTICLE 10

Exemption from Restrictions and Prohibitions

Goods imported or exported for the Official Activities of the Secretariat shall be exempt from any prohibitions or restrictions applicable to such goods on grounds of national origin.

ARTICLE 11

Re-sale

Goods which have been acquired or imported by the Secretariat to which exemptions under Article 9 above apply and goods acquired or imported by the Executive Secretary or other staff members to which the exemptions under Article 16 or Article 17 below apply, shall not be given away, sold, lent, hired out or otherwise disposed of in the Argentine Republic, except under conditions agreed in advance with the Government.

ARTICLE 12

Currency and Exchange

The Secretariat shall be exempt from any currency or exchange restrictions, including those in respect of funds, currency and securities received, acquired, held or disposed of. The Secretariat may also operate without restrictions bank or other accounts for its official use in any currency, and have them transferred freely within the Argentine Republic or to any other country.

ARTICLE 13

Communications

1.   With regard to its official communications and the transfer of all its documents, the Secretariat shall enjoy treatment not less favourable than that generally accorded by the Government to any other government, including the latter's diplomatic mission, in the matter of priorities, rates and taxes on mails and all forms of telecommunications.

2.   The Secretariat may employ any appropriate means of communication, including encrypted messages. The Government shall not impose any restriction on the official communications of the Secretariat or on the circulation of its publications.

3.   The Secretariat may install and use radio transmitters with the consent of the Government.

4.   Official correspondence and other official communications of the Secretariat are not subject to censorship and shall enjoy all the guarantees established by Argentine domestic law.

ARTICLE 14

PUBLICATIONS

The importation and exportation of the Secretariat's publications and other information material imported or exported by the Secretariat within the scope of its Official Activities shall not be restricted in any way.

ARTICLE 15

PRIVILEGES AND IMMUNITIES OF DELEGATES

1.   Delegates of the States Parties shall enjoy, during their stay in the Argentine Republic for exercising their official functions, the privileges and immunities of diplomatic agents as established in the Vienna Convention on Diplomatic Relations of 18 April 1961.

2.   The provisions of paragraph 1 above shall be applicable irrespective of the relations existing between the governments which the persons referred to represent and the Government, and are without prejudice to any additional immunities to which such persons may be entitled in the Argentine Republic.

3.   The privileges and immunities described in paragraph 1 above shall not be accorded to any delegate of the Government or to any national or permanent resident of the Argentine Republic.

4.   The Government shall treat Delegates with all due respect and shall take all necessary measures to prevent encroachment on their person, freedom and dignity. Where it appears that an offence may have been committed against a Delegate, steps shall be taken in accordance with Argentine legal procedures to investigate the matter and to ensure that appropriate action is taken with respect to the prosecution of the alleged offender.

ARTICLE 16

EXECUTIVE SECRETARY

In addition to the privileges, immunities, exemptions and facilities provided for in Article 17 below, the Executive Secretary, unless he or she is a national or a permanent resident of the Argentine Republic, shall enjoy the privileges, immunities, exemptions and facilities to which a diplomatic agent in the Argentine Republic is entitled, including privileges, immunities, exemptions and facilities in respect of the members of their family which form a part of the household, unless they are nationals or permanent residents of the Argentine Republic.

ARTICLE 17
STAFF MEMBERS

1. Staff members of the Secretariat:

    (a) shall have, even after the termination of their service with the Secretariat, immunity from suit and any other legal or administrative proceedings or judicial request in respect of acts and things done by them in the exercise of their official functions, including words written or spoken;

    (b) immunities set out in the sub-paragraph above shall not, however, apply in the case of a motor vehicle offence committed by such a staff member or the Executive Secretary nor in the case of civil or administrative proceedings arising out of death, damage or personal injury caused by a motor vehicle belonging to or driven by him or her to the extent that compensation is not recoverable from insurance;

    (c) shall be exempt from any obligations in respect of military service and all other kinds of mandatory service, unless they are nationals or permanent residents of the Argentine Republic;

    (d) shall be exempt from the application of laws relating to the registration of aliens and immigration;

    (e) unless they are nationals or permanent residents of the Argentine Republic, they shall be accorded the same exemption from currency and exchange restrictions as is accorded to an official of comparable rank from an international agency in the Argentine Republic;

    (f) unless they are nationals or permanent residents of the Argentine Republic, they shall when taking up their post in the Argentine Republic for the first time, be exempt from customs duties and other such charges (except payments for services) in respect of import of furniture, motor vehicles and other personal effects in their ownership or possession or already ordered by them and intended for their personal use or for their establishment. Such goods shall be imported within six months of a staff member's first entry into the Argentine Republic but in exceptional circumstances an extension of this period shall be granted by the Government. Goods which have been acquired or imported by staff members and to which exemptions under this sub-paragraph apply shall not be given away, sold, lent, hired out, or otherwise disposed of except under conditions agreed in advance with the Government. Furniture and personal effects may be exported free of duties when leaving the Argentine Republic on the termination of the official functions of the staff member;

(g) shall be exempt from all taxes on income received from the Secretariat. This exemption shall not apply to staff members who are nationals or permanent residents of the Argentine Republic;

(h) shall have similar repatriation facilities as are accorded to representatives of international agencies in times of international crisis; and

(i) shall have personal inviolability with respect to any form of personal arrest or detention or seizure of their personal baggage unless they are nationals or permanent residents of the Argentine Republic.

2.   Privileges and immunities applicable to a staff member in accordance with sub-paragraphs c), d), e), f), h) and i) of paragraph 1 above shall also apply to the members of his or her family forming a part of the household, unless they are nationals or permanent residents in the Argentine Republic.

ARTICLE 18
EXPERTS

In the exercise of their functions experts shall enjoy the following privileges and immunities to the extent necessary for the carrying out of their functions, including while traveling in the Argentine Republic to that effect:

(a) immunity from suit and any other legal or administrative proceedings or judicial request in respect of acts and things done by them in the exercise of their official functions, including words written or spoken. This immunity shall not, however, apply in the case of a motor vehicle offence committed by such experts nor in the case of civil or administrative proceedings arising out of death, damage or personal injury caused by a motor vehicle belonging to or driven by him or her to the extent the compensation is not recoverable from insurance. Such immunity shall continue after the expert's function in relation to the Secretariat has ceased;

(b) inviolability for all their official papers and documents as well as other official materials, which are related to the performance of the functions of the Secretariat;

(c) unless they are nationals or permanent residents of the Argentine Republic, the same exemption from currency and exchange restrictions as is accorded to a representative of a foreign Government on a temporary mission in Argentina on behalf of that Government; and

(d) unless they are nationals or permanent residents of the Argentine Republic, immunity from personal arrest and detention and from attachment of personal luggage.

ARTICLE 19
VISAS

1.   All persons having official business with the Secretariat, namely Delegates and members of their families forming a part of the household, staff members of the Secretariat and any members of their families forming a part of the household, and the experts referred to in Article 18 above, shall have the right of entry into, stay in and exit from the Argentine Republic.

2.   The Government shall take all measures necessary to facilitate the entry into the Argentine Republic, the sojourn on that territory and the exit therefrom of all persons mentioned in paragraph 1 above. Visas, where required, shall be granted without wait or delay, and without fee, on production of a certificate that the applicant is a person described in paragraph 1 above. In addition, the Government shall facilitate travel for such persons within the territory of the Argentine Republic.

ARTICLE 20
COOPERATION

The Secretariat shall co-operate fully at all times with the appropriate Authorities in order to prevent any abuse of the privileges, immunities and facilities provided for in this Agreement. The Government reserves its sovereign right to take reasonable measures to preserve security. Nothing in this Agreement prevents the application of laws necessary for health and quarantine or, with respect to the Secretariat and its officials, laws relating to public order.

ARTICLE 21
NOTIFICATION OF APPOINTMENTS, IDENTITY CARDS

1.   The ATCM shall notify the Government of the appointment of an Executive Secretary and the date when he or she is to take up or relinquish the post.

2.   The Secretariat shall notify the Government when a staff member takes up or relinquishes his or her post or when an expert starts or finishes a project or mission.

3.   The Secretariat shall twice a year send to the Government a list of all experts and staff members and the members of their families forming a part of the household in the Argentine Republic. In each case the Secretariat shall indicate whether such persons are nationals or permanent residents of the Argentine Republic.

4.   The Government shall issue to all staff members and experts as soon as practicable after notification of their appointment, a card bearing the photograph of the holder and identifying him or her as a staff member or expert as the case may be. This card shall be accepted by the appropriate Authorities as evidence of identity and appointment. The members of their families forming a part of the household shall also be issued with an identity card. When the staff member or expert relinquishes his or her duties, the Secretariat shall return to the Government his or her identity card together with identity cards issued to members of his or her family forming a part of the household.

ARTICLE 22
CONSULTATION

The Government and the Secretariat as an organ of the ATCM shall consult at the request of either of them concerning matters arising under this Agreement. If any such matter is not promptly resolved, the Secretariat shall refer it to the ATCM.

ARTICLE 23
AMENDMENT

This Agreement may be amended by agreement between the Government and the ATCM.

ARTICLE 24
SETTLEMENT OF DISPUTES

Any dispute arising out of the interpretation or application of this Agreement shall be settled by consultation, negotiation or any other mutually acceptable method, which may include resort to binding arbitration.

ARTICLE 25
ENTRY INTO FORCE AND TERMINATION

1.   This Agreement shall enter into force upon signature.

2.   This Agreement may be terminated by written notification by either Party. Termination shall take effect two years after receipt of such notification unless otherwise agreed.

Done in Punta del Este, on the tenth day of May, two thousand and ten, in two originals, in the Spanish, English, French and Russian languages, both being equally authentic.

<table>
<tr><td>For the Argentine Republic</td><td>For the Antarctic Treaty
Consultative Meeting</td></tr>
<tr><td>Jorge Enrique Taiana
Minister of Foreign Affairs,
International Trade and Worship</td><td>Roberto Puceiro Ripoll
Chairman of the XXXIII Antarctic
Treaty Consultative Meeting</td></tr>
</table>

ANNEX TO DECISION 2 (2021)
STAFF REGULATIONS FOR THE SECRETARIAT
OF THE ANTARCTIC TREATY

REGULATION 1
PREAMBLE

1.1   These Staff Regulations establish the fundamental principles of employment, regulate the working relationships and establish the rights and duties of members of the staff of the Secretariat of the Antarctic Treaty (the Secretariat), and includes the staff members who render their services in and receive remuneration from the Antarctic Secretariat.

1.2   In the text of these Staff Regulations, reference to staff members in the masculine gender shall apply to staff members of both sexes, unless it is clearly inappropriate from the context to do so.

REGULATION 2
DUTIES, OBLIGATIONS AND PRIVILEGES

2.1   Staff members, upon accepting their appointments, shall pledge themselves to discharge their duties faithfully and to conduct themselves solely with the interests of the ATCM in mind. Their responsibilities as staff members are not national but are exclusively owed to the ATCM.

2.2   Staff members shall at all times conduct themselves in a manner in keeping with the Antarctic Treaty. They shall always bear in mind the loyalty, discretion and tact imposed on them by their responsibilities in the performance of their duties. They shall avoid all actions, statements or public activities which might be detrimental to the ATCM and its aims.

2.3   Staff members are not required to renounce either their national feelings or their political or religious convictions, but must ensure that such views or convictions do not adversely affect their official duties or the interests of the ATCM. Staff members shall uphold the highest standards of efficiency, competence, and integrity. The concept of integrity includes, but is not limited to, probity, impartiality, fairness, honesty, and truthfulness in all matters affecting their work and status.

2.4   In the performance of their duties, staff members may neither seek nor accept instructions from any government or authority other than the ATCM.

2.5   Staff members shall observe maximum discretion regarding official matters and shall abstain from making private use of information they possess by reason of their position. Authorisation for the release of information for official purposes shall lie with the ATCM or the Executive Secretary, as the case may require.

2.6   Staff members shall, in general, have no employment other than with the Secretariat. In special cases, staff members may accept other employment, provided that it does not interfere with their duties in the Secretariat, and that prior authorisation by the Executive Secretary has been obtained. The ATCM's prior authorisation shall be obtained in respect of the Executive Secretary.

2.7   No staff member may be associated in the management of a business, industry or other enterprise, or have a financial interest therein if, as a result of the official position held in the Secretariat, he/she may benefit from such association or interest. Ownership of non-controlling stock in a company shall not be considered to constitute a financial interest within the meaning of this Regulation.

2.8   Staff members shall enjoy the privileges and immunities granted to them under the Headquarters Agreement for the Secretariat of the Antarctic Treaty, pursuant to Article 5 of Measure 1 (2003) of ATCM XXVI.

REGULATION 3
HOURS OF WORK

3.1   The normal working day shall be eight hours, Monday to Friday, for a total of forty hours per week.

3.2   The Executive Secretary shall establish the working hours, and may alter them for the benefit of the ATCM, as circumstances may require.

3.3   Staff members may work flexible hours in accordance with the Flextime System included in the internal procedures, with the approval of the Executive Secretary and in the interest of the functioning of the Secretariat.

3.4   Full-time staff members shall take a lunch break of no less than 30 minutes and no longer than 1 hour, to be taken no later than five hours after beginning the working day.

REGULATION 4
CLASSIFICATION OF STAFF

4.1   Staff members shall be classified in either of the two following categories:

(a)   Executive Category

Positions of high responsibility of an executive nature. These posts will be filled by appropriately qualified professionals, preferably with University qualifications or the equivalent. Staff members in this category will be recruited internationally but only among nationals of Consultative Parties.

(b)   General Staff Category

All other staff, such as translators, interpreters, technical, administrative and auxiliary positions. Such staff members shall be recruited in Argentina from among nationals of Consultative Parties.

4.2   Persons employed under Regulation 11 shall not be classified as staff members.

REGULATION 5
SALARIES AND OTHER REMUNERATION

5.1   The scale of salaries for staff members in the executive category is attached in Schedule A. The salaries of staff members in the executive category shall be paid in US currency.

5.2   The scale of salaries for staff members in the general category is attached in Schedule B. The salaries of staff members in the general category shall be paid in US currency.

5.3   For the purposes of these regulations the term 'dependent' means:

(a)   any unsalaried child, who is born of, or adopted by, a staff member, his/her spouse, or their children, who is below the age of eighteen years and who is dependent on a staff member for main and continuing support;

(b)   any child fulfilling the conditions laid down in paragraph (a) above, but who is between eighteen and twenty five years of age and is receiving school or university education or vocational training;

(c)   any handicapped child who is dependent on a staff member for main and continuing support;

(d)   any other child who is given a home by and is dependent on a staff member for main and continuing support;

(e)   any member of the family forming part of the household of the staff member, for whose main and continuing support a staff member is legally responsible.

5.4   The salaries of staff members in the executive category shall begin at Step 1 of the level at which they are appointed. They shall remain at that level for at least the first year of employment.

5.5   The promotion of the Executive Secretary and other staff members from one level to another requires the prior approval of the ATCM.

5.6   The Executive Secretary shall seek to make arrangements for any staff member in the executive category whose salary is subject to income tax in his/her home country, to be reimbursed for that tax. Such arrangements shall be made only on the basis that the direct costs of reimbursement are paid by the staff member's home country. Staff members in the general category will be responsible for the payment of income tax, if any on their salaries in their home country.

5.7   Staff members shall receive annual step increases, subject to satisfactory performance of their duties. Step increases shall cease once the staff member has reached the highest step in the level in which he/she is serving.

5.8   Only in very special cases, on the proposal of the Executive Secretary and with the approval of the ATCM, may a staff member in the executive category be appointed at a salary higher than Step 1 of the relevant level.

5.9   Staff members in the executive category are not entitled to overtime pay or compensatory leave.

5.10 Staff members in the general category required to work more than 40 hours during one week will be compensated, at the discretion of the Executive Secretary:

(a)   with compensatory leave equivalent to hours of overtime performed; or

(b)   by remuneration per overtime hour, to be calculated at the rate of time and a half, or if the additional time is worked on a Sunday, or on holidays listed in Regulation 7.8, at the rate of double time.

5.11 The ATCM shall pay duly justified representation expenses incurred by the Executive Secretary in the performance of his/her duties within the limits prescribed annually in the budget.

5.12 With the prior approval of the Executive Secretary, an employee in the general services category who must carry out all the duties of an employee of a higher classification for a period of a minimum of four weeks shall be paid the salary of the corresponding higher category while carrying out these tasks.

REGULATION 6
RECRUITMENT AND APPOINTMENT

6.1 In accordance with Article 3 of Measure 1 (2003), the ATCM shall appoint an Executive Secretary and shall establish the remuneration and such other entitlements as it deems appropriate. The Executive Secretary's term of office shall be for four years unless otherwise decided by the ATCM and the Executive Secretary shall be eligible for reappointment for one additional term. The total length of employment may not exceed eight years.

6.2 In accordance with Article 3 of Measure 1 (2003) the Executive Secretary shall appoint, direct, and supervise other staff members. The paramount consideration in the appointment, transfer or promotion of staff members shall be the need to secure the highest standards of efficiency, competence and integrity. Qualifications being equivalent, gender and geographic balance will be taken into account when selecting candidates. Subject to this, due consideration should be given to recruiting Executive staff on as wide a basis as possible from among the nationals of Consultative Parties.

6.3 Upon selection, each staff member shall receive an offer of appointment stating:

(a)   that the appointment is subject to these regulations and to changes which may be made to them from time to time;
(b)   the nature of the appointment including a description of the duties and tasks of the position;
(c)   the date on which the staff member is required to commence duty and the working hours;
(d)   the period of appointment, the notice required to terminate it and the period of probation;
(e)   for executive staff the period of appointment, which shall not exceed four years, and which may be renewed in consultation with the ATCM;

(f)   the category, level, commencing rate of salary and the scale of steps increases and the maximum salary attainable;

(g)   the allowances attached to the appointment;

(h)   any special terms and conditions which may be applicable.

6.4   Together with the offer of appointment, staff members shall be provided with a copy of these Regulations. Upon acceptance of the offer staff members shall sign the relevant Work Contract and state in writing that they are familiar with and accept the conditions set out in these Regulations.

6.5   The Executive Secretary shall carry out an annual evaluation of the performance of the staff member's duties, using a recognised method, to ensure the continued improvement of management, as well as to facilitate consideration of the promotion of, or justify the separation from the service of, the staff member.

REGULATION 7
LEAVE

7.1   Staff members shall be entitled to 25 paid work days of annual leave during each working year of service, or for periods of less than a full calendar year at the rate of two paid work days for each completed month of service. Said leave shall be divided into 15 paid work days for holiday leave, which may be taken consecutively, and 10 additional paid work days that shall be taken in periods of no more than 3 days. Annual holiday leave is cumulative, but at the end of each calendar year, not more than 15 workdays may be carried over to the following year. Additional leave is not cumulative.

7.2   The taking of leave shall not cause undue disruption to normal Secretariat operations. In accordance with this principle, leave dates and duration shall be subject to the needs of the ATCM. Leave dates shall be approved by the Executive Secretary who shall, as far as possible, bear in mind the personal circumstances, needs and preferences of staff members.

7.3   Annual leave may be taken in one or more periods. Staff members shall inform the Executive Secretary of their intention to take holiday leave at least four weeks in advance after verifying with other staff members that such leave would not result in an overlap that might affect the normal functioning of the Secretariat.

7.4   Any absence not approved within the terms of these Regulations shall be deducted from annual leave.

7.5   Staff members who, upon termination of their appointment, have accumulated annual leave which has not been taken shall receive the cash equivalent estimated on the basis of the last salary received to a limit of 30 days.

7.6   After 18 months of service the Secretariat shall, in accordance with Regulations 9.3 and 9.4, pay fares to the staff member's home country on annual leave for internationally recruited staff members and their dependents. Following this, home leave fares shall be granted at two-year intervals provided that:

(a)   dependents who benefit from this grant have resided at Buenos Aires for at least 6 months prior to travel;

(b)   it is expected that staff members will return to the Secretariat to continue rendering their services for a minimum additional period of 6 months.

7.7   The possibility of combining travel to home country on leave with official travel in Secretariat service may also be considered provided the functions of the Secretariat are not disadvantaged.

7.8   Staff members shall be entitled to the holidays and non-working days established by law and/or decree by the Argentine Republic and/or the City of Buenos Aires, i.e.:

Fixed Holidays

1 January	New Year's Day
24 March	National Holiday
02 April	National Holiday
01 May	National Holiday
25 May	National Holiday
9 July	National Holiday
8 December	Immaculate Conception
25 December	Christmas Day

Moveable Holidays and Non-Work Days

	Monday and Tuesday of Carnival Holy Thursday
	Good Friday
17 June	National Holiday
20 June	National Holiday
17 August	National Holiday
12 October	National Holiday

20 November   National Holiday

7.9   If under special circumstances members of the staff are required to work on one of the aforementioned days, or if any one of the above holidays falls on a Saturday or Sunday, the holiday shall be observed on another day to be set by the Executive Secretary, who shall take into account the efficient functioning of the Secretariat.

7.10 Staff members shall be entitled to the following special leave: 1

a)   For marriage: 10 consecutive days;
b)   For the death of a spouse, domestic partner, children or parents: 3 consecutive days;
c)   For the death of siblings, parents-in-law or grandparents: 1 day;
d)   For moving house: 2 days;
e)   For sitting an exam at second or university level: 2 consecutive days per exam, with a maximum of 10 days per calendar year;
f)   To care for, due to illness, the employee's spouse, parents or children: 2 days, unless at the Executive Secretary's discretion and for justified reasons a longer time period is granted.

7.11 Following twelve months of continued employment in the Secretariat staff may request unpaid leave for personal reasons of up to a maximum of three months. Such leave shall not cause undue disturbance to the normal functioning of the Secretariat. Under this stipulation, the dates and duration of the leave shall be subject to the approval of the Executive Secretary.

7.12 Staff members shall not be granted sick leave for a period of more than three consecutive days or more than a total of seven working days in any calendar year without a medical certificate.

7.13 (a) Staff members shall be granted certified sick leave for an accident or non-occupational illness in accordance with the provisions of the current legal regime in the Argentine Republic.

(b) In the event that the accident or illness prevents a staff member from fulfilling his/her duties with the Secretariat, the staff member and his/her dependents shall be

____

[1] Regulations 7.10, 7.11 and 7.14 are established in accordance with prevailing Argentine national law; the ATCM should review any significant change in Argentine national law but may at any time review these provisions.

entitled to return travel and expenses for relocating to his/her country of origin or former residence at the expense of the Secretariat.

7.14 Staff members shall be entitled to maternity leave as provided by the current legal regime in the Argentine Republic. On the other hand, the father shall receive 10 days of paid leave that may be used in the same period described above.

7.15 After twelve months of continuous employment in the Secretariat, staff members shall be entitled to parental leave of up to three months of unpaid leave for the birth or adoption of a child.

REGULATION 8
SOCIAL SECURITY

8.1 Staff members will be responsible for the full payment of their personal Social Security contributions. The Secretariat will make all employer contributions to Social Security and will pay any mandatory insurance corresponding to the employer, as provided by the regulations of the Argentine Republic.

8.2 In the event of the death of a staff member, their dependents will be entitled to a death allowance and payment of the return trip and moving expenses to their country of origin or previous residence by the Secretariat, regardless of any compensations to which they may be entitled by the regulations of the Argentine Republic and those mentioned in Article 10.

8.3 Eligibility of the dependents of a deceased staff member for the payment of return travel and removal expenses shall lapse if the travel is not undertaken within six months of the date of the staff member's death.

8.4 The above mortality allowance for death shall be calculated in accordance with the following scale:

Years of Service	Months of Gross Salary Following Death
Less than 3 years	3 months
3 years and more, but less than 7 years	4 months
7 years and more, but less than 9 years	5 months
9 years and more	6 months

8.5   The Secretariat shall pay for customary and reasonable expenses for shipment of the staff member's body from the place of death to the place designated by the next of kin.

REGULATION 9
TRAVEL

9.1   Staff members may be required to undertake travel, including international travel, on behalf of the Secretariat. All official travel shall be authorised by the Executive Secretary in advance within the limits of the budget, and the itinerary and travelling conditions shall be those best suited for maximum effectiveness in the fulfilment of duties assigned.

9.2   With regard to official travel, a reasonable travel allowance shall be paid in advance for accommodation and daily living expenses.

9.3   Economy class shall be utilised, wherever feasible, for air travel. For journeys over nine hours in flying time, business class may be utilised.

9.4   First class may be utilised for land travel, but not for travel by sea or air.

9.5   Following completion of a journey for official purposes, staff members shall repay any travel allowances to which, in the event, they were not entitled. Where staff members have incurred expenses above and beyond those for which travel allowances have been paid, they shall be reimbursed, against receipts and vouchers, as long as such expenses were necessarily incurred in pursuit of their official duties.

9.6   On taking up an appointment in the Executive Category staff members shall be eligible for:

(a)   payment of air fares (or equivalent) and travel allowance for themselves, their spouses and dependents to Buenos Aires;

(b)   payment of removal costs, including the shipment of personal effects and household goods from place of residence to Buenos Aires, subject to a maximum volume of 30 cubic metres or one international standard shipping container;

(c)   payment or reimbursement of sundry other reasonable expenses related to relocation, including insurance of goods in transit and excess baggage charges. Such payments shall be subject to prior approval by the Executive Secretary.

9.7   Staff members who, in the course of their duty, are required to use private motor vehicles for official travel purposes shall, with the prior authorisation of the Executive Secretary, be entitled to receive a reimbursement of the reasonable costs involved. The costs associated with normal daily travel to and from the place of work shall not be reimbursed.

REGULATION 10
SEPARATION FROM SERVICE

10.1 Staff members may resign at any time upon giving three months' notice or such lesser period as may be approved by the Executive Secretary (in the case of staff other than the Executive Secretary) or the ATCM (in the case of the Executive Secretary).

10.2 In the event of a staff member resigning without giving the required notice the Executive Secretary (in the case of staff members other than the Executive Secretary) or the ATCM (in the case of the Executive Secretary) reserves the right to decide whether repatriation expenses or any other allowance shall be paid.

10.3 Appointment of staff members may be terminated upon prior written notice at least three months in advance, by the Executive Secretary (and in the case of the Executive Secretary by the ATCM) when this is deemed to be for the benefit of the efficient functioning of the Secretariat due to restructuring of the Secretariat or if it is considered that the staff member does not give satisfactory service, fails to comply with the duties and obligations set out in these Regulations, or is incapacitated for service.

10.4 In the event of separation from service with the Secretariat, executive staff members shall be compensated at a rate of one month base pay for each year of service, beginning the second year, unless the cause of termination has been gross dereliction of duties imposed in Regulation 2.

10.5 In the event of involuntary separation from service of a member of the general services staff, compensation will be paid in accordance with the regulations of the Argentine Republic. If the cause of termination has been a gross dereliction of the duties mentioned in Regulation 2, or having incurred in offences established as very serious in Regulation 12, said compensation will not be granted.

10.6 On separation from service, an executive staff member shall be entitled to the following:

(a)   payment of economy class air fares (or equivalent) to the staff member's country of origin or former residence, for the staff member and dependent members of his/her family; and

(b)   payment of removal costs, including the shipment of personal effects and household goods from place of residence in Buenos Aires to the country of origin or former residence, subject to a maximum volume of 30 cubic metres or one international shipping container.

10.7 Any member of staff shall be entitled to end his/her relationship with the Secretariat in order to take retirement, with advance notice of three (3) months from the date of the termination.

10.8 The Executive Secretary may request that a staff member take retirement benefit, provided that said staff member has met the requirements to obtain retirement benefit established by Law in the Argentine Republic. Prior notice to this effect shall be given and the working relationship shall be maintained for one year from said notice. Upon expiry of that period, the fully binding working relationship shall be deemed terminated.

REGULATION 11
TEMPORARY PERSONNEL UNDER CONTRACT

11.1 The Executive Secretary may contract temporary personnel necessary to discharge special duties of a short-term nature in the service of the Secretariat. Short term shall be defined as a contract lasting less than six months. Such personnel shall be classified as additional help and may be paid on an hourly basis.

11.2 Persons in this category may include additional translators, interpreters, typists, and other persons contracted for meetings, as well as those whom the Executive Secretary contracts for a specific task.

REGULATION 12
DISCIPLINARY REGIME

12.1 The Executive Secretary may apply disciplinary sanctions to staff members for any non-compliance that is registered and depending on its severity. Said sanctions will be duly notified to whoever has committed the disciplinary offence.

The Executive Secretary shall provide the staff member with:

(a) The allegations of misconduct in writing or by electronic means, which should include the specific obligations or standards of conduct that the staff member has breached;

(b) Notification of the staff member's right to respond to the allegations of misconduct and to provide any evidence within a 3 working day period.

12.2 Three types of disciplinary offences are established, which may be sanctioned according to their severity. These are:
- Minor offences. These may be sanctioned with a warning.
- Serious offences. These may be sanctioned with a warning or 1 to 4 days suspension without pay.
- Very Serious offences. These may be sanctioned with 5 to 10 days suspension without pay or with fair dismissal.

12.3 Sanctionable offences will be listed in the Internal Regulation on Disciplinary Regime of the Secretariat, highlighting that said list is not expected to be comprehensive and shall leave non-listed actions that deserve to be sanctioned at the discretion and analysis of the Executive Secretary.

REGULATION 13
APPLICATION AND AMENDMENT OF REGULATIONS

13.1 The Executive Secretary is responsible for the administration of these Staff Regulations on behalf of the ATCM. The ATCM shall determine their applicability to the Executive Secretary.

13.2 Any doubts arising from application of these Regulations shall be resolved by the Executive Secretary following consultation with the ATCM.

13.3 All matters not foreseen in these Regulations shall be brought to the attention of the ATCM by the Executive Secretary.

13.4 These Regulations, including the schedules, may be amended by a Decision of the ATCM.

Salary Scale FY 2021/22

Schedule A

SALARY SCALE FOR THE EXECUTIVE STAFF

(United States Dollar)

2021/22							STEPS									
Level		I	II	III	IV	V	VI	VII	VIII	IX	X	XI	XII	XIII	XIV	XV
E1	A	$ 135 302	$ 137 819	$ 140 337	$ 142 855	$ 145 373	$ 147 890	$ 150 407	$ 152 926							
E1	B	$ 169 127	$ 172 274	$ 175 421	$ 178 569	$ 181 716	$ 184 863	$ 188 009	$ 191 158							
E2	A	$ 113 932	$ 116 075	$ 118 218	$ 120 359	$ 122 501	$ 124 642	$ 126 783	$ 128 926	$ 131 069	$ 133 211	$ 135 352	$ 135 595	$ 137 709		
E2	B	$ 142 415	$ 145 093	$ 147 772	$ 150 449	$ 153 126	$ 155 802	$ 158 479	$ 161 158	$ 163 837	$ 166 513	$ 169 190	$ 169 494	$ 172 136		
E3	A	$ 95 007	$ 97 073	$ 99 140	$ 101 207	$ 103 275	$ 105 341	$ 107 408	$ 109 476	$ 111 542	$ 113 608	$ 115 675	$ 116 915	$ 118 154	$ 120 193	$ 122 231
E3	B	$ 118 758	$ 121 341	$ 123 925	$ 126 509	$ 129 094	$ 131 676	$ 134 260	$ 136 845	$ 139 427	$ 142 010	$ 144 594	$ 146 143	$ 147 693	$ 150 242	$ 152 788
E4	A	$ 78 779	$ 80 693	$ 82 609	$ 84 518	$ 86 435	$ 88 347	$ 90 257	$ 92 174	$ 94 089	$ 96 000	$ 97 915	$ 98 448	$ 100 336	$ 102 223	$ 104 110
E4	B	$ 98 474	$ 100 866	$ 103 262	$ 105 648	$ 108 044	$ 110 434	$ 112 822	$ 115 217	$ 117 611	$ 119 999	$ 122 393	$ 123 060	$ 125 419	$ 127 778	$ 130 137
E5	A	$ 65 315	$ 67 029	$ 68 739	$ 70 452	$ 72 162	$ 73 873	$ 75 586	$ 77 293	$ 79 007	$ 80 719	$ 82 427	$ 82 981			
E5	B	$ 81 644	$ 83 786	$ 85 924	$ 88 065	$ 90 203	$ 92 342	$ 94 482	$ 96 617	$ 98 759	$ 100 899	$ 103 034	$ 103 726			
E6	A	$ 51 706	$ 53 351	$ 54 994	$ 56 641	$ 58 284	$ 59 928	$ 61 575	$ 63 219	$ 64 862	$ 65 862	$ 66 508				
E6	B	$ 64 632	$ 66 689	$ 68 742	$ 70 801	$ 72 855	$ 74 910	$ 76 969	$ 79 024	$ 81 078	$ 82 328	$ 83 135				

Note: Row B is the base salary (shown in Row A) with an additional 25% for salary on-costs (retirement fund and insurance premiums, installation and repatriation grants, education allowances etc.) and is the total salary entitlement for executive staff in accordance with regulation 5.1.

Schedule B

SALARY SCALE FOR THE GENERAL STAFF

(United States Dollar)

Level		I	II	III	IV	V	VI	STEPS VII	VIII	IX	X	XI	XII	XIII	XIV	XV
G1		$ 64 788	$ 67 810	$ 70 834	$ 73 856	$ 77 006	$ 80 291									
G2		$ 53 990	$ 56 508	$ 59 028	$ 61 546	$ 64 172	$ 66 909									
G3		$ 44 990	$ 47 089	$ 49 189	$ 51 288	$ 53 477	$ 55 760									
G4		$ 37 493	$ 39 242	$ 40 991	$ 42 741	$ 44 564	$ 46 466									
G5		$ 30 972	$ 32 419	$ 33 863	$ 35 310	$ 36 818	$ 38 391									
G6		$ 25 388	$ 26 571	$ 27 756	$ 28 941	$ 30 177	$ 31 465									
G7		$ 13 724	$ 14 317	$ 14 911	$ 15 505	$ 16 124	$ 16 770									

Note: Updated versions are adopted regularly as a part of the Secretariat's Programme and Budget.

FINANCIAL REGULATIONS FOR THE SECRETARIAT OF THE ANTARCTIC TREATY

REGULATION 1
APPLICABILITY

1.   These Regulations shall govern the financial administration of the Secretariat of the Antarctic Treaty (the Secretariat) established under Measure 1 (2003) of the XXVI ATCM (the Measure).

REGULATION 2
FINANCIAL YEAR

2.   The financial year shall be for 12 months commencing 1 April and ending 31 March, both dates inclusive.

REGULATION 3
THE BUDGET

3.1   A draft budget comprising estimates of receipts by the Secretariat and of expenditures by the Secretariat shall be prepared by the Executive Secretary for the ensuing financial year.

3.2   The draft budget shall include a statement of significant financial implications for subsequent financial years in respect of work programs presented by the ATCM in terms of administrative, recurrent and capital expenditure.

3.3   The draft budget shall be divided by functions into items and, where necessary or appropriate, into sub-items.

3.4   The draft budget shall be accompanied by details both of the appropriations made for the previous year and estimated expenditure against those appropriations, together with such supporting documents as may be required by Parties or deemed necessary or desirable by the Executive Secretary. The precise form in which the draft budget is to be presented shall be prescribed by the ATCM.

3.5   The Executive Secretary shall submit the draft budget to all Consultative Parties of the ATCM at least 60 days prior to the ATCM. At the same time, and in the same form as the draft budget, the Executive Secretary he shall prepare and submit to all Consultative Parties a forecast budget for the subsequent financial year.

3.6   The draft budget and the forecast budget shall be presented in United States currency.

3.7   At each annual meeting, the ATCM shall adopt the budget for the Secretariat. The budget shall be treated as a matter of substance and approved by a representative of all Consultative Parties present at the meeting. In determining the size of the budget the ATCM shall adhere to the principle of cost-effectiveness.

REGULATION 4
APPROPRIATIONS

4.1   The appropriations adopted by the ATCM shall constitute an authorisation for the Executive Secretary to incur obligations and make payments for the purposes for which the appropriations were adopted and up to the amounts so adopted.

4.2   All forward commitments shall be identified in annual budgets presented to the ATCM. Unless the ATCM decides otherwise, the Executive Secretary may incur obligations against future years before appropriations are adopted when such obligations are necessary for the continued effective functioning of the Secretariat, provided such obligations are restricted to administrative requirements of a continuing nature not exceeding the scale of such requirements as authorised in the budget of the current financial year. In other circumstances the Executive Secretary may incur obligations against future years only as authorised by the ATCM.

4.3   Appropriations shall be available for the financial year to which they relate. At the end of the financial year all appropriations shall lapse. Commitments remaining undischarged against previous appropriations at the end of a financial year shall be carried over and be included in the budget for the next financial year, unless the ATCM otherwise decides.

4.4   The Executive Secretary may make transfers within each of the main appropriation lines of the approved budget. The Executive Secretary may also make transfers between such appropriation lines up to 15 per cent of the appropriation lines. All such transfers must be reported by the Executive Secretary to the next annual meeting of the ATCM. The transfers authorised under these regulations shall not result in overall increase of the budget above that approved by the ATCM, nor will they result in increased expenditure in future years.

4.5   The ATCM shall prescribe the conditions under which unforeseen and extraordinary expenses may be incurred.

REGULATION 5
PROVISION OF FUNDS

5.1   On approval of the budget for a financial year, the Executive Secretary shall send a copy thereof to all Consultative Parties notifying them of their contributions and the date they are due, and requesting them to remit their contributions due.

5.2   All contributions shall be made in United States currency.

5.3   Contribution from States that become Consultative Parties after the beginning of the financial period shall be made *pro rata temporis* for the balance of the financial period.

5.4   The Executive Secretary shall acknowledge pledges and contributions immediately upon receipt. The Executive Secretary shall report to each meeting of the ATCM on the receipt of contributions and the status of any arrears.

5.5   Contributions shall be due for payment on the first day of the financial year (i.e. the due date) and shall be paid not later than 90 days after that date. However, in the case referred to in Regulation 5.3, contributions by a new Consultative Party shall be made within 60 days following the date on which its accession becomes effective.

REGULATION 6
FUNDS

6.1   (a)   There shall be established a General Fund for the purpose of accounting for the income and expenditure of the Secretariat;

(b)   contributions paid by Consultative Parties pursuant to Article 4 of Mcasure 1 (2003) under and Miscellaneous Income as referred to in Regulation 7.1 shall be credited to the General Fund;

(c)   an advance made by a Consultative Party shall be carried to the credit of the Party which has made the advance.

6.2   (a)   There shall be established a Working Capital Fund in an amount of not more than one-sixth (1/6) of the budget of that financial year to ensure continuity of operations in the event of a temporary shortfall of cash and for other purposes to be determined by the ATCM from time to time. The Working Capital Fund shall initially be financed up to the specified level by a transfer from the General Fund, and thereafter from the fund determined appropriate by the Antarctic Treaty Consultative Meeting;

(b)   advances made from the Working Capital Fund to finance budgetary appropriations during a financial year shall be reimbursed as soon as possible, and to the extent that income is available for that purpose;

(c)   income derived from the investment of the Working Capital Fund shall be credited to Miscellaneous Income of the General Fund; and

(d) trust and Special Funds may be established by the Secretariat at the direction of the ATCM for the purpose of receiving funds and making payments for purposes not covered by the General or Working Capital Fund of the Secretariat. The purposes and limits of each Trust and Special Fund shall be clearly defined by the ATCM. Unless otherwise provided by the ATCM, such Funds shall be administered in accordance with the present regulations.

6.3 The Secretariat shall notify the Consultative Parties of any cash surplus in the General Fund at the close of the financial year that is not required to meet undischarged commitments and of each Consultative Party's proportional share of that surplus. Those Parties that choose not to allow their portion of the surplus to be retained in the General Fund shall notify the Secretariat of that fact and shall have that portion credited against such Consultative Parties' contributions for the following year. Otherwise any cash surplus shall be retained in the General Fund.

6.4. Where contributions are received from new Consultative Parties after the commencement of the financial year and such contributions have not been taken into account in formulating the budget these shall be placed in the General Fund.

REGULATION 7
OTHER INCOME

7.1 All income other than contributions to the budget under Regulation 5, income derived from investment in the Working Capital Fund as provided in Regulation 6.2 (c), and that referred to in Regulation 7.5 below, shall be classified as Miscellaneous Income and credited to the General Fund.

7.2 Profits and losses on exchange shall be credited and debited to Miscellaneous Income.

7.3 The use of Miscellaneous Income shall be subject to the same financial controls as activities financed from regular budget appropriations.

7.4 Voluntary contributions above and beyond Consultative Parties' budget contributions may be accepted by the Executive Secretary provided that the purposes for which the contributions are made are consistent with the policies, aims and activities of the ATCM. Voluntary contributions offered by non-Consultative Parties and non-Parties may be accepted, subject to agreement by the ATCM that the purposes of the contribution are consistent with the policies, aims and activities of the ATCM.

7.5 Voluntary contributions as referred to in Regulation 7.4 above shall be treated as Trust or Special Funds under Regulation 6.2(d).

REGULATION 8

CUSTODY OF FUNDS

8.1   The Executive Secretary shall designate a bank or banks in which the funds of the Secretariat shall be kept and shall report the identity of the bank or banks so designated to the ATCM.

8.2   (a)   The Executive Secretary may make short-term investments of moneys not needed for the immediate requirements of the Secretariat. Such investments shall be restricted to securities and other investments issued by institutions or Government bodies with current ratings, provided by a rating body approved by the Secretariat's auditor and indicating a strong capacity to pay. The details of investment transactions and income derived shall be reported in the documents supporting the budget.

(b)   With regard to moneys held in Trust or Special Funds for which use is not required for at least 12 months, longer-term investments may be authorised by the ATCM provided such action is consistent with the terms under which the moneys were lodged with the Secretariat. Such investments shall be restricted to securities and other investments issued by institutions or Government bodies with current ratings, provided by a rating body approved by the Secretariat's auditor and indicating a strong capacity to pay.

8.3   Income derived from investments shall be credited to the Fund from which the investment was made.

REGULATION 9

INTERNAL CONTROL

9.1   The Executive Secretary shall:

(a)   establish detailed financial rules and procedures after consultation with the external auditor to ensure effective financial administration and the exercise of economy in the use of funds and effective custody of the physical assets of the Secretariat;

(b)   cause all payments to be made on the basis of supporting vouchers and other documents which ensure that the goods or services have been received and that payment has not previously been made;

(c)   designate officers who may receive moneys, incur obligations and make payments on behalf of the Secretariat; and

(d)   maintain and be responsible for internal financial control to ensure:

    (i)   the regularity of the receipt, custody and disposal of all funds and other financial resources of the Secretariat;

    (ii)   the conformity of obligations and expenditures with the appropriations adopted by the ATCM; and

    (iii)   the economic use of the resources of the Secretariat.

9.2   No obligations shall be incurred until allotments or other appropriate authorisations have been made in writing under the authority of the Executive Secretary.

9.3   The Executive Secretary may propose to the ATCM, after full investigation by him/her, the writing off of losses of assets, provided that the external auditor so recommends. Such losses shall be included in the annual accounts.

9.4   Tenders in writing for equipment, supplies and other requirements shall be invited by advertisement, or by direct requests for quotation from at least three persons or firms able to supply the equipment, supplies, or other requirements, if such exist, in connection with all purchases or contracts, the amounts of which exceed USD2,000. For amounts exceeding USD500, but less than USD2,000 competition shall be obtained either by the above means or by telephone or personal enquiry. The foregoing rules, shall, however, not apply in the following cases:

(a)   where it has been ascertained that only a single supplier exists and that fact is so certified by the Executive Secretary;

(b)   in case of emergency, or where, for any other reason, these rules would not be in the best financial interests of the Secretariat, and that fact is so certified by the Executive Secretary.

REGULATION 10
THE ACCOUNTS

10.1 The Executive Secretary shall ensure that appropriate records and accounts are kept of the transactions and affairs of the Secretariat and shall ensure that all payments out of the Secretariat's moneys are correctly made and properly authorised. The Executive Secretary shall also ensure that adequate control is maintained over the assets of, or in the custody of, the Secretariat and over the incurring of liabilities by the Secretariat.

10.2 The Executive Secretary shall submit to the Consultative Parties, as soon as practicable but not later than 30 June immediately following the end of the financial year, annual financial statements showing, for the financial year to which they relate:

(a)   the income and expenditure relating to all funds and accounts;

(b)   the situation with regard to budget provisions, including:

    (i)   the original budget provisions;

    (ii)   the approved expenditure in excess of the original budget provisions;

    (iii)   any other income;

    (iv)   the amounts charged against these provisions and other income;

(c)   the financial assets and liabilities of the Secretariat;

(d)   details of the performance of the investments; and

(e)   writing off of losses of assets proposed in accordance with Regulation 9.3.

10.3 The Executive Secretary shall also give such other information as may be appropriate to indicate the financial position of the Secretariat. These financial statements shall be prepared in a form approved by the ATCM after consultation with the external auditor.

10.4 The accounting transactions of the Secretariat shall be recorded in the currency in which they took place but the annual financial statements shall record all transactions in United States currency.

10.5 Appropriate separate accounts shall be kept for all Working Capital, Special and Trust Funds.

REGULATION 11
EXTERNAL AUDIT

11.1 The ATCM shall appoint an external auditor who shall be the Auditor- General or equivalent statutory authority from a Consultative Party of the ATCM and shall serve for a term of two years with the possibility of re-appointment. The ATCM will ensure the external auditor's independence of the Secretariat, and the Secretariat's staff. The ATCM shall fix the terms of office, appropriate funds to the external auditor and may consult him/her on the introduction or amendment of any financial regulations or detailed accounting methods as well as on all matters affecting auditing procedures and methodology.

11.2 The external auditor or a person or persons authorised by him/her shall be entitled at all reasonable times to full and free access to all accounts and records of the Secretariat relating directly or indirectly to the receipt or payment of moneys by the Secretariat or to the acquisition, receipt, custody or disposal of assets by the Secretariat. This applies also to allowances such as travel and representation expenses. The external auditor or a person or persons authorised by him/her may make copies of or take extracts from any such accounts or records.

11.3 If required by the ATCM to perform a full audit, the external auditor shall conduct his/her examination of the statements in conformity with generally accepted auditing standards and shall report to the ATCM on all relevant matters, including:

(a)   whether, in his/her opinion, the statements are based on proper accounts and records;

(b)   whether the statements are in agreement with the accounts and records;

(c)   whether, in his/her opinion, the income, expenditure and investment of moneys and the acquisition and disposal of assets by the Secretariat during the year have been in accordance with these Regulations; and

(d)   observations with respect to the efficiency and economy of the financial procedures and the conduct of business, the accounting system, internal financial controls and the administration and management of the Secretariat.

11.4 If required by the ATCM to perform a review audit, the external auditor shall review the statements and accounting controls in operation. The external auditor shall report to the ATCM whether anything has come to his/her attention which would cause him/her to doubt whether:

(a)   the statements are based on proper accounts and records;

(b)   the statements are in agreement with the accounts and records; or

(c)   the income, expenditure and investment of moneys and the acquisition and disposal of assets by the Secretariat during the year have been in accordance with these Regulations.

11.5 The Executive Secretary shall provide the external auditor with the facilities he/she may require in the performance of the audit.

11.6 The Executive Secretary shall provide to the Parties of the ATCM a copy of the audit report and the audited financial statements within 30 days of their receipt.

11.7 The ATCM shall, if necessary, invite the external auditor to address the Meeting and to attend discussions on any item under scrutiny and consider recommendations arising out of his/her findings.

REGULATION 12

ACCEPTANCE OF ANNUAL FINANCIAL STATEMENTS

12.1 The ATCM shall, following consideration of the audited annual financial statements and audit report submitted to the Consultative Parties under Regulation

11 signify its acceptance of the audited annual financial statements or take such other action as it may consider appropriate.

REGULATION 13
INSURANCE

13.1 The Secretariat shall take out suitable insurances with one or more reputable financial institution against normal risks to its assets.

REGULATION 14
GENERAL PROVISION

14.1 These Regulations may be amended by a Decision of the ATCM.

14.2 Where the ATCM is considering matters which may lead to a decision which has financial or administrative implications, it shall have before it an evaluation of those implications from the Executive Secretary.

MEASURE 1 (2003)
SECRETARIAT OF THE ANTARCTIC TREATY

The Representatives,

Recalling the Antarctic Treaty and the Protocol on Environmental Protection to the Antarctic Treaty (the Protocol);

Recognizing the need for a secretariat to assist the Antarctic Treaty Consultative Meeting (the ATCM) and the Committee for Environmental Protection (the CEP) in performing their functions;

Recalling Decision 1 (2001) of the XXIV ATCM on the establishment of the Secretariat of the Antarctic Treaty (the Secretariat) in Buenos Aires, Argentina;

Recommend to their Governments the following Measure for approval in accordance with paragraph 4 of Article IX of the Antarctic Treaty:

ARTICLE I
SECRETARIAT

The Secretariat shall constitute an organ of the ATCM. As such it shall be subordinated to the ATCM.

ARTICLE II
FUNCTIONS

1.   The Secretariat shall perform those functions in support of the ATCM and the CEP which are entrusted to it by the ATCM.

2.   Under the direction and supervision of the ATCM, the Secretariat shall, in particular:

(a)   Provide, with assistance from the host government, secretariat support for meetings held under the Antarctic Treaty and the Protocol and other meetings in conjunction with the ATCM. Secretariat support shall include:

(i)   Collation of information for ATCM/CEP meetings e.g. environmental impact assessments and management plans;

    (ii)   preparatory work for and distribution of the meeting agendas and reports;

    (iii) translation of meeting documents;

    (iv) provision of interpretation services;

    (v)   copying, organizing and distributing meeting documents; and

    (vi) assisting the ATCM, in drafting the meeting documents including the final report;

(b)   support intersessional work of the ATCM and the CEP by facilitating the exchange of information, organizing meeting facilities and providing other secretariat support as directed by the ATCM;

(c)   facilitate and coordinate communications and exchange of information amongst Parties on all exchanges required under the Antarctic Treaty and the Protocol;

(d)   under guidance from the ATCM, provide the necessary coordination and contact with other elements of the Antarctic Treaty system and other relevant international bodies and organizations as appropriate;

(e)   establish, maintain, develop and, as appropriate publish, databases relevant to the operation of the Antarctic Treaty and the Protocol;

(f)   circulate amongst the Parties any other relevant information and disseminate information on activities in Antarctica;

(g)   record, maintain and publish, as appropriate, the records of the ATCM and CEP and of other meetings convened under the Antarctic Treaty and the Protocol;

(h)   facilitate the availability of information about the Antarctic Treaty system;

(i)   prepare reports on its activities and present them to the ATCM;

(j)   assist the ATCM in reviewing the status of past Recommendations and Measures adopted under Article IX of the Antarctic Treaty;

(k)   under the guidance of the ATCM, take responsibility for maintaining and updating an Antarctic Treaty system "Handbook"; and

(l)   perform such other functions relevant to the purposes of the Antarctic Treaty and the Protocol as may be determined by the ATCM.

ARTICLE III

EXECUTIVE SECRETARY

1.   The Secretariat shall be headed by an Executive Secretary who shall be appointed by the ATCM from among candidates who are nationals of Consultative

Parties. The procedure for the selection of the Executive Secretary shall be determined by a Decision of the ATCM.

2. The Executive Secretary shall appoint staff members essential for the carrying out of the functions of the Secretariat and engage experts as appropriate. The Executive Secretary and other staff members shall serve in accordance with the procedures, terms and conditions set out in the Staff Regulations which shall be adopted by a Decision of the ATCM.

3. During the intersessional periods the Executive Secretary shall consult in a manner to be prescribed in the Rules of Procedure.

ARTICLE IV
BUDGET

1. The Secretariat shall operate in a cost-effective manner.

2. The budget of the Secretariat shall be approved by the Representatives of all Consultative Parties present at the ATCM.

3. Each Consultative Party shall contribute to the budget of the Secretariat. One half of the budget shall be contributed equally by all Consultative Parties. The other half of the budget shall be contributed by the Consultative Parties based on the extent of their national Antarctic activities, taking into account their capacity to pay.

4. The method for calculating the scale of contributions is contained in Decision 1 (2003) and the Schedule attached to it. The ATCM may amend the proportion in which the abovementioned two criteria shall apply and the method for calculating the scale of contributions by means of a Decision.

5. Any Contracting Party may make a voluntary contribution at any time.

6. Financial Regulations shall be adopted by a Decision of the ATCM.

ARTICLE V
LEGAL CAPACITY AND PRIVILEGES AND IMMUNITIES

1. The legal capacity of the Secretariat as an organ of the ATCM as well as its privileges and immunities and those of the Executive Secretary and other staff members in the territory of the Argentine Republic shall be provided for in the Headquarters Agreement for the Secretariat of the Antarctic Treaty (the Headquarters Agreement) hereby adopted and annexed to this Measure, to be concluded between the ATCM and the Argentine Republic.

2.   The ATCM hereby authorizes the person who holds the office of the Chair to sign the Headquarters Agreement on its behalf at the time this Measure becomes effective.

3.   The Secretariat may exercise its legal capacity as provided for in Article 2 of the Headquarters Agreement only to the extent authorized by the ATCM. Within the budget approved by and in accordance with any other decision of the ATCM, the Secretariat is hereby authorized to contract, and to acquire and dispose of movable property in order to perform its functions as set out in Article 2 of this Measure.

4.   The Secretariat may not acquire or dispose of immovable property or institute legal proceedings without the prior approval of the ATCM.